WORDS ⬛

—It is never nece⬛⬛⬛⬛ ⬛⬛⬛ spiritual growth with elaborate rituals. Simple
  honest prayers constantly uttered, sincerity,
  faith, and love are all the ingredients
  one needs.
—Have love toward all things, and many joys
  will be yours.
—Follow your hunches and intuition, for it
  will be us whispering in your ear with
  God's message.
—Only your soul has substance and remains
  alive and functioning forever.
—From where you are, your view is not as expansive as ours. We can see beyond the
  bend of the lane, whereas you see only the
  part of the path as you look at your feet.
—Peace cannot manifest in the world until Divine Peace, Divine Love, is realized in
  each soul.

SPIRIT GUIDES

ANGELS IN THE ARMY OF GOD

Spirit Guides
Angels in the Army of God

Norma Kalina

A SIGNET BOOK

SIGNET
Published by the Penguin Group
Penguin Books USA Inc., 375 Hudson Street,
New York, New York 10014, U.S.A.
Penguin Books Ltd, 27 Wrights Lane,
London W8 5TZ, England
Penguin Books Australia Ltd, Ringwood,
Victoria, Australia
Penguin Books Canada Ltd, 10 Alcorn Avenue,
Toronto, Ontario, Canada M4V 3B2
Penguin Books (N.Z.) Ltd, 182–190 Wairau Road,
Auckland 10, New Zealand

Penguin Books Ltd, Registered Offices:
Harmondsworth, Middlesex, England

First published by Signet, an imprint of Dutton Signet,
a division of Penguin Books USA Inc.

First Printing, July, 1997
10 9 8 7 6 5 4 3 2 1

 REGISTERED TRADEMARK—MARCA REGISTRADA

Printed in the United States of America

Foreword

Now, . . . there might be someone for you. . . . I heard a voice so loud and clear (while seated at the hotel piano) that I turned to my bass player and asked, "What did you say?" He looked at me as though I were crazy; his reply . . . "I didn't say anything . . . what are you talking about?"

It was this voice so loud and clear in my ear . . . "my Spirit Guide" advising me as I watched Norma (talking to some people at a nearby table) that she indeed would be the "one."

And so it began (more than thirty years ago) . . . my wonderful adventure/love affair with my soulmate, Norma, in her most recent incarnation on this earth plane.

"There might be someone for you" . . . the understatement of all time! Norma Jane Vandervort Partlow Kalina.

An incredible woman, journalist, author, artist,

poet, lyricist, teacher and student of life (both here and hereafter)—spiritual counselor to literally scores of people. She was the complete Renaissance woman, also managing to be a professional singer, actress, fashion model, "great wife," phenomenal mom, fantastic grandmother, and as she liked to put it, M.C. in a jazz club in Philadelphia . . . whew!!!

Norma learned on November 14, 1995, that her book *Spirit Guides—Angels in the Army of God* was about to be published. Thus, having completed her mission on this earth on December 3, 1995, she returned to heaven to become one of those "Angels in the Army of God" herself.

We all love her and miss her so very much—the sadness that I feel at her passing can only be surpassed by the joy in heaven at her return. . . .

—Ron Kalina

Introduction

❧

Ancient cultures, as well as many of those down through the centuries, include recognition of reincarnation, the belief that when the mortal body dies, the soul lives on eternally, passing to another plane or higher dimension, (heaven, nirvana, astral plane, happy hunting ground, etc.) until the return to a new embodiment here on the planet Earth or elsewhere.

Allegorically, the soul passes from the earthly school to the astral school where it is further educated in the process of attainment of the ultimate goal, graduation to at-one-ment with God, the Creator, Divine Mind, and Creative Energy Force of the Universe.

A particular segment of the curriculum for a discarnate soul involves tutoring those souls matriculating in the earthly school in mortal manifestation while nurturing its own spiritual growth.

Some human students refute the teaching, do not believe the "school of life" concept, become truant, disinterested, and drop out of their spiritual education. Other mortal students, after some bewilderment during orientation, gradually realize what school (life on Earth) is all about and eagerly listen to their teachers. Those teachers, or more aptly student teachers, are Spirit Guides, also called angels.

Without wishing to seem facetious, I would describe the master guide (a highly evolved soul who oversees certain of the discarnate souls) as the school Principal and God as the One and Only Superintendent over all the schools, all the Principals, all the teachers, and all the students.

If you think back to your various teachers throughout your childhood, you may remember a few as very serious, others stern, some playful and humorous, and still others a combination of all the above.

So it is with Spirit Guides. They can cause raucous laughter with their witticism and inspire awe with their great philosophical depth. They reprimand and praise, give encouragement, dispense wise instructions, and issue commands.

All counseling and instructions given by the guides are presented with love and sincere concern for the spiritual growth of not only the particular medium but of all mankind. The guides eagerly await the awakening of each mortal to his or her spiritual heritage and ask nothing more than belief, faith, and love. My guides call themselves "God's disciples" and are anxious to be recognized so as to facilitate their assignment of helping human beings learn about God and His Divine Plan.

I have lovingly dubbed my guides "the kids," which seems inappropriately frivolous until one learns that Robert Louis Stevenson called his guides "brownies" and relied on them for the plot of his next story, which he insisted could not have been written without their assistance.

My Spirit Guides channel their teaching through automatic writing, although I consider myself far from being a totally developed psychic. Through the years I tended my soul the best I knew how, but I had not the slightest hint of psychic ability nor did I recognize that every person on Earth is psychic. It is a matter of degree of development and of being aware of the possible dangers (mentioned later in this book), taking steps to avoid those inherent perils, and developing and maintaining the God-given powers within each of us.

My life here on Earth, since the Spirit Guides ultimately attracted my attention, has expanded into an incredible world of joy, love, purpose, direction, abundance, truth, knowledge, blessings, and happiness which know no bounds. In their messages my guides constantly urge me to spread the word and "tell the world about us."

Thus I introduce you to William, Van, Mother, Ondaras, and a continuing parade of my Spirit Guides.

Chapter 1

One night in the early summer of 1972, as I drove from Paoli toward a town with the charming name of King of Prussia, a wild storm swept across eastern Pennsylvania. Jagged lightning split open the clouds, dumping rain on the countryside as though from giant cauldrons. Peering through the inadequate sweeps of the windshield wiper, I tried to find the pavement stripes so I could at least stay in my own lane.

Traffic on this main highway leading to the Schuykill Expressway and the toll booths of the Pennsylvania Turnpike was, fortunately, below normal, but now and then a speeding maniac passed me, splattering great globs of water over the windshield. Leaning forward and gripping the steering wheel with white-knuckled hands, I strained my eyes for a glimpse of the lane makers, alert to any cars that might be in front of me.

Suddenly, like the news bulletin released in lights around the New York Times building, the words AC-CIDENT AHEAD marched swiftly, letter-by-letter across the inside of my forehead. Startled, I lifted my foot from the accelerator but did not brake. What was happening here? Where had the warning come from and why? Was I imagining the warning? Had I lost my mind?

Before I could reason out any answers, I saw tail-lights zigzag crazily about 20 yards ahead in my lane. Lightly tapping my brakes to prevent a skid, I watched in horror as a terrifying scene, lit as bright as day by repeated streaks of lightning, unfolded before me. The errant car whirled in a complete circle, smashed into the divider wall, bounced back, and flipped over on its top in the middle of the lane in which I was driving.

Had I not lifted my foot from the gas pedal when I did, I would have crashed into the other car. I avoided the accident only because of the advanced "news bulletin" I had received. When I arrived home I told my husband that my guardian angels must have been watching over me.

Three years before that mystifying psychic experience, I had been a disbeliever in reincarnation and a skeptic concerning psychic phenomena. At that time I discovered the many books about Edgar Cayce, the noted psychic who gave amazing life readings while in a trance. On my birthday that same year, I was given a book authored by Ruth Montgomery, the professional journalist who claimed to be a medium via automatic writing for messages from her Spirit Guide. Interesting reading. Very provocative. I decided to open my rigid mind, accept the accounts at face value, and delve into further study.

It did not occur to me then that perhaps I, too, could contact Spirit Guides. Psychic experiences happened to other people, special people, not an ordinary housewife. Even on learning of the Patience Worth series written automatically over many years by a housewife, I did not believe it possible for me and I put the thought from my mind, content to experience psychic phenomena vicariously.

Several years after my near accident in Pennsylvania, having read dozens of books on psychic phenomena, I came across a tiny pamphlet on how to approach automatic writing. Well, I mused, if guardian angels hovered near other people, perhaps one or two were flying around my area. As instructed by the pamphlet I sat with pencil tip poised on a pad of paper. Agonizing hours crawled by as I concentrated prayerfully, humbly asking God for some sign of a spirit guide, some legible word or message.

Each session produced wriggly lines that appeared to have been drawn by a two-year-old child. I could decipher no word at all and felt as though I were scrutinizing the erratic trail of an earthworm. An Aries has very little patience but in this instance I was determined to persevere. Each night I went through the same routine of praying with the pencil touching the paper expectantly. Each night I was rewarded with a series of loops, squiggles, and an occasional scratch which could be read as an *r* or an *m* if I squinted. Then, after several days of our two-hour stints, just as I felt prone to giving up, the word *yes* appeared. Greatly encouraged, I sat at the table for an hour or so daily, more determined than ever to make further contact. In a week the breakthrough came with the sentence *"Wm love no joy."* I was elated, for, in spite of the slanted childish scrawl, I recognized the words. *"Wm love no joy."* But what did they mean?

That same week, while still pondering that message and the few others I had received, a respected friend directed me to a notable psychic, a very spiritual lady who for many years has channeled through the Ouija board. She was only five years old when her family became aware of her strong psychic powers. Wisely they nurtured her along instead of exploiting or denying her gift.

The psychic, whom I shall call Lola, did not know me nor did she know my friend except for one meeting years before, a meeting Lola could scarcely recall. At the beginning of my first appointment with Lola, I told her nothing of my past nor did I tell her of my attempts at automatic writing.

Amazingly, Lola immediately received messages.

Her hand flew back and forth across the board as she spoke.

"I am William and I am your guide. We send blessings and joy to you."

William! Of course, *Wm* is an abbreviation for William!

Lola's hand stopped and she looked at me. "Ask a question," she said quietly.

Experience with psychic phenomena was new to me, and I trembled with anticipation and wonder. I asked, "Did I know the spirit, William, who is sending these messages, in this lifetime?"

Lola's hand went into action immediately. "Yes, positively," she intoned. "I was your mailman and your husband was mean to you. He shouted at you and said terrible things to you. He was not at all nice to you. We are so happy that you are now happy and we bless you and send love."

My hands flew to my mouth to stifle a gasp as tears sprang to my eyes. My God, I had known William during my first marriage when I lived in Texas. He had indeed been our mailman and undoubtedly had heard some of our domestic arguments. The mailbox hung in the front of the house, directly under the kitchen window, a window left open the majority of the time, for we enjoyed moderate weather.

Without explaining my reaction to Lola, I asked who my other guides might be. Quickly she answered, "Van, who is a strong adviser to you, and Mother, who protects you when you are driving, walking, or traveling anywhere. She takes good care of you."

Noticing the astonished look on my face and the tears quivering on my eyelids, Lola compassionately inquired, "Do those names mean something to you?"

I merely nodded my head, unable for the moment to speak, for she had just corroborated names being received in my writing. When finally able to control my emotions, I told Lola of the automatic writing and of three early messages.

The second message I received was this: *"I am mother my love to you an Ron joy."* You can imagine the tearful elation with which I greeted that message. My mother, a dear sweet loving woman who passed on in 1955, was one of my guides! And she knew of my second husband whom I met more than twelve years later! Lola had just substantiated the name of another of my guides.

As I now told Lola, my third day's session of automatic writing had produced the following from William: *"Van sends love an [sic] many joys."* When I asked William the identity of Van, the writing, shaky and lopsided, read: *"Me your Daddy love Norma."*

The next day a garbled message came through, one which made no sense at all. When I asked for clarification, William interceded with: *"Van says he not mas-*

ter words yet." I chuckled as I read the explanation. It sounded so much like my father.

Daddy passed on in 1975 at the age of 82. His coworkers called him Van but he was always Daddy to me. It seemed strange he would use Van in his transmission to a daughter he called "Punkin" to the end of his days. In this life he had been a bricklayer who consistently had trouble with English grammar, much to the consternation of my genteel mother who was the society editor of our small-town weekly newspaper.

Prior to Lola's reading she knew none of this. When she confirmed the names of William, Van, and Mother without a hint from me, any doubts I might have harbored about the validity of automatic writing, Lola's credence as a psychic, or the existence of Spirit Guides were burned away in an instant. I knew then I was not fantasizing or imagining the messages into manifestation through emotional will. I left Lola's home carrying with me the realization of the magnitude of what she had told me and my responsibilities concerning automatic writing. I offered a humble prayer of thanks and asked that more be revealed to me that I might go in the proper direction with my automatic writing and with furthering my spiritual growth.

Thus began a joyous though sometimes puzzling adventure with the daily involvement and guidance of my small band of spirit guides.

In the beginning I heard nothing, no "inner voice." I focused my mind on God, concentrated on God and rhythmic deep breathing and the pencil began to move. At that time my guides not only spelled out many words phonetically (*no* for *know*) they also did not dot *i*'s nor cross *t*'s. Early on they used *u* for the word *you*, *r* for *our* and *are*, and did not add *d* to the word *and*. Nor was there punctuation of any kind; one sentence ran into the next.

Occasionally capital letters were used but only for proper names, never at the beginning of a sentence. For the most part I have added punctuation to their early writing for this manuscript (for easier reading and comprehension). Later, however, they began transmitting with punctuation, proper capital letters, and indented paragraphs.

The handwriting initially resembled that of a five-year-old. As the weeks went by the writing subtly changed; it became smaller, more legible, and marched along in a fairly straight line. But the tenor of the messages remained the same for quite a while—a mixture of pidgin English and that of the American Indian. In one instance a guide poetically used "long tears" to signify great sorrow. On a day I became angry at the inefficient service of a travel agency, an order from the guides came to "'lower your mad."

The guides also can be very firm with me. Many times they insisted I was to write several books, yet when I made inquiries as to subject matter and starting date, Van chided me for my impatience and advised, *"You learn first and study many things. Learn more of love and truth."*

In another session William warned, *"You are not ready yet. Learn more of truth and love to tell the world of us."* When I asked a third time about the books, I received this message, much more fluent than any I had received previously: *"You must obey William now first, Love, Ondaras."* Ondaras? Who was this interloper? Not trusting myself to ask the guides, I made an appointment with Lola.

"Is there maybe some kind of leader, a head honcho, of my group of guides?" I inquired, not mentioning the message from Ondaras.

As her hands flew back and forth across the board Lola translated, "Hondarus is your master guide. You knew him in at least one lifetime centuries ago in Europe where he was a street-corner philosopher. He wore a tall black hat, a long black coat, and carried a book under his arm. You were one of his most devoted followers."

This was indeed more information than I had asked for, but the visual image of this apparently astute soul who had sent the stern message delighted me.

Astounded at Lola's accuracy I asked for the spelling of the name. Lola consulted the board. "Hon-da-rus." She spelled out the word.

When I spelled Ondaras from my writing, Lola suggested that according to whatever nationality he may have been in any given lifetime perhaps the *H* was silent in the pronunciation and I was getting the name phonetically from my guides, an explanation entirely plausible under the circumstances.

In that first message from Ondaras he chastised me for being impatient when I had been told to learn more. I meekly complied and ceased any further questioning about the proposed books.

Many questions whirled in my mind, however. Statistically, the years I have lived stretch over two-thirds of my projected life span. Why had my spirit guides not attempted to get in touch with me earlier? Or had they? Had Spirit Guides tried to get my attention only to have me ignore them? To find the answer I turned back the clock of memory. As your basic slightly overweight, suburban housewife with family responsibilities and the spiritual background of a dogmatic, small-town Midwesterner, I was ill-equipped, mentally or emotionally, to come face-to-face with psychic phenomena of even the mildest sort.

With a demanding husband and two lively sons, I lacked the time and the inclination to indulge in contemplations of a metaphysical nature even if I had been aware.

The thoughts tumbling over each other in my head ran more along the lines of dirty laundry, house cleaning, weed-infested flower beds, football, swimming meets, P.T.A., church choir, sinus headaches, and homework. My mind stretched no further than planning all the Cub Scout den meetings for our pack, organizing the programs for the P.T.A., juggling the logistics of the family dental and medical appointments, and trying to remember whose turn it was to feed the dog and cat.

During my childhood I somehow picked up the belief that if you were good you went to heaven when you died, a heaven above the bright blue sky where beautiful angels with sparkling halos sat on white clouds playing golden harps around a huge gateway encrusted with silver, gold, and pearls. If you were bad, after your death you went to hades and dwelt in a fiery furnace around which danced a maniacal devil who held a pitchfork in his hands, laughing diabolically, elated that you could never escape the flames. Whichever path you chose during your life, when you died your soul dwelt forever in either a definitive heaven or an equally definitive hell, unless, of course, your transgressions were judged of a minor nature. Then, you hovered in purgatory until your soul decided which direction it would take for eternity.

Please do not misunderstand. Never would I belittle the religion that plays a dominant role in my life even today. My words serve only to set the scene for what follows. Simply stated, the organized confined religion of my childhood did not fully prepare me for the expansive communion with the Holy Spirit I have been privileged to experience in recent years.

Or am I wrong? As I sit at the computer trying to explain to the reader, and to myself, why I eventually recognized and accepted psychic phenomena, reincarnation, and the guidance of spiritual entities, I realize that all which went before in the religious atmosphere of my childhood, restricted or not, was all a part of my spiritual "basic training." Because of that stable, albeit narrow, religious atmosphere and the installation of an unshakable faith in God, I see now I have been building toward a much deeper spiritual understanding. I know now I was being conditioned by the Holy Spirit to be ready when the big steps came. Were it not for my solid religious foundation, a vital stepping stone to further spiritual growth, it is doubtful I would have been able, with my personal human intellect, to discern the broader scope of my life's purpose or, if you will, each of my lives' purposes. Nor would I have been able to cope with the monumental revelations opening to me each day, each hour. Without proper preparation, the appearance of spirit guides in my life would have certainly frightened me.

In searching my past I suddenly recalled a remarkable event that surely signaled the presence of my angel guides. In October 1976, my older son, who lived in Texas, called to tell us he would be flying to

Los Angeles to spend the weekend with us, and asked if I could pick him up at the airport at nine the following night.

Just before leaving for the airport the next evening, I put a pot of water on the stove, and left a note for my husband instructing him to turn on the stove to heat the water when he arrived home from his job at 9:45. Having the water hot would enable me to prepare the spaghetti dinner more quickly when my son and I arrived home.

Happily I pulled out of the garage. Less than a half block from our apartment a firm voice said, "Go back!" The voice startled me, so I slowed down and wondered why I had received the warning. Had I automatically turned on the stove without thinking? Mentally I retraced my movements. No, I had not turned on the stove, of that I was positive. As I accelerated the car to continue on my way, the voice boomed louder, demanding, "GO BACK!"

I obeyed immediately. If I were mistaken and had turned the stove on unconsciously, my negligence might start a fire. Better to be safe than sorry. I retraced my path, parked the car in the garage, climbed the stairs to our apartment, unlocked the door, turned on the kitchen light, and was relieved to see the stove was off. "Now, why was I ordered to go back?" I questioned aloud to no one in particular.

In a short time, as I once again headed for the airport, the answer came. On the San Diego Freeway near

Mulholland Drive, in the southbound lane I was traveling, a terrible accident had occurred less than ten minutes before at just the time I would have been driving in that spot had I not heeded the warning to go back.

As I sat in stalled traffic at the accident site, shaking in awe and teary-eyed relief, I leaned my head on the steering wheel and gratefully voiced my loving thanks in one of the most sincere prayers of my life.

Remembering that night, it now amuses me to imagine my angels jumping with joy at my having heeded their call.

The third such episode a few months later included Ron, my husband, who was at the wheel of our car as we drove south on the Hollywood Freeway. As is my infernal habit, I directed him from the passenger side. He often teasingly asks if, in addition to my regular driver's license, do I also have one for side-seat driving?

"Go over in the next lane, honey," I ordered, "so we can avoid the access road to the other freeway."

Ron made no verbal response nor was there any physical indication he had heard my command.

"Ron!" I cried impatiently. "Why don't you go over—"

At that moment a car flew past us at a speed we later estimated to be at least seventy miles an hour. The speeding car cut all the way across our lane in front of us, missing our car by no more than two inches as it sped into the access lane and out of sight onto the Ventura Freeway.

After a few seconds of meaningful silence I said quietly, "I'm glad you didn't follow my orders. We would have been killed."

When he could find his voice, Ron answered in an awed tone, "I couldn't! I tried to turn the wheel when you asked me, but it just wouldn't move!"

We glanced at each other wide-eyed.

"It just wouldn't move!" he repeated in wonder as he now steered us into the proper lane. "Something was driving for me." His voice was hushed and reverent.

My only answer was, "Yes."

Spirit Guides hovered around me long before I knew of them. From the day we are born, they are with each of us attempting to be recognized so they can carry on their work in what they call the "university of the soul."

It occurred to me to wonder who might have been my guides prior to Mother's passing in 1955. William's soul departed sometime during the 1960s and my father's in 1975. Surely some guiding spirit counseled and protected me from my birth until the angel called "Mother" took over.

When I put the question to William, he answered, *"Ondaras, of course, has been with you in other lives but in this one only as your master guide. Your grandfather assumed a role in your guidance the instant of your birth two years after he came to this level. Others you knew several lives back. They elected to help you as part of their growth project.*

"A childhood friend, who passed from fever when a young girl, took up the task for a while."

This bit of news startled me for Amelia had not entered my thoughts for several decades. I was twelve years old and she, a neighbor, nearly sixteen when she succumbed to scarlet fever. Since grades seven through twelve were housed in the same building, Amelia and I walked the mile to school together every day. Because of the disparity in our ages, Amelia and I were not playmates nor social friends, but I remember her as sweet and kind and helpful with advice on any problem that confronted me. How nice that she continued looking after me during my teen years, but I hadn't known.

The guides continued with the answer to my question about early guides. *"Other of your ancestors from many generations back guided you gently and lovingly until they deemed it time to reincarnate, then others took up the vigil.*

"So you see, loved one, you have always had us walking beside you although you did not recognize the signs," William continued. *"There were times when we were sure you were close then realized you needed a bit more time. You recognized our messages from time to time and heeded them but you knew not from whence they came."*

The explanation more than satisfied my curiosity and I established a daily pattern of contact with "the kids"—my Spirit Guides—William, Van, Mother, and Ondaras.

Chapter 2

My father, born in 1893, lived for eighty-two years and for nearly all of those years was an avid student of the lore of the American Indian. As a child he talked with the aged people of the area of southern Ohio where he lived and, with rapt attention, listened to the tales told of their personal experiences with the natives, the Shawnee in particular because the tribe was the most prevalent in Ohio.

During his lifetime my father voraciously studied every book about Indians he could lay his hands on and traveled far and wide to libraries and museums for additional information. On yellow school tablets (the kind with a drawing of an Indian chief printed on the cover), he kept a chronicle of Indian events and stories as he learned or read of them. At his passing, after years of writing, he had accumulated enough lore to fill an entire closet with boxes of the tablets.

Through the years he traipsed through miles of countryside marking the Indian foot trails known as traces which crisscross our country. In his later years he lectured and exhibited Indian artifacts to civic groups and school children, demonstrating how to build a tepee and how to start a fire with two shards of flint rock and a few twigs.

"He must have been an Indian once," my mother remarked many times, although the subject of reincarnation had never been discussed in our household that I recall. Daddy could say several Indian words and phrases; he knew the customs and lifestyles indigenous to the myriad tribes and Indian nations of the United States.

Lola, the psychic, informed me that I had been an American Indian at least twice in other incarnations—once as a Seminole along the Florida coast where I fell in love with a French sailor, and in another lifetime as a Sioux near the Dakota border where the Mississippi has its source.

The reminiscence of my happy childhood includes riding bareback on my pinto pony into the hills behind our farmhouse pretending to be an Indian maiden and living (only for a day) on teaberry leaves, sassafras bark, and clear pure water from a spring near a cave.

Thus, after the initial shock of realizing my father, Van, was one of my Spirit Guides, I was not totally surprised when Indian-like phrases cropped up in my early writing.

"If a man chooses wrong way to go instead of follow light," Van wrote, *"he find only long tears* [great sorrow] *this time and lose love and joy and much success."*

Another of Van's early messages, ignoring anything resembling correct English grammar, stated, *"Ondaras say you make young friend you talk with have good things in mind and soul. He get much in small* [short] *time."*

In the beginning of the automatic writing I could always sense when Van was dictating the message. *"You make book. We much glad you tell others. You much good to obey and learn truth."* If I listened very carefully, I could hear tom-toms echoing in the air.

Lest you think I have been unduly influenced by Ruth Montgomery's *A Search for the Truth,* I swear I had not yet read the book, not until a year later. In the book she states that most spiritualists in the United States believe each of us has an American Indian as a Spirit Guide.

Two of my friends who are not acquainted have each heard from the spirit of an Indian named White Cloud as did Montgomery in a seance she attended. Van is the closest thing to an American Indian that appeared in my writing.

In correspondence with one of my newfound friends who contacts her guides daily, I asked if her guides each seem to have a certain style to their transcriptions. She answered, "As of today forty-four different guides have entered (in seven years of writing). Each one has a similar message but each has an entirely different style so I can recognize their personalities as they start to write. However, each guide seems to be a step higher or cover still another facet of life—rabbi, minister, poet, writer, a military man, and two politicians who came daily one summer then left. But each had a different style."

As Van became more articulate and I more receptive, the Indian phrases faded, yet a certain nuance came through his writing which I recognized, just as I knew when Mother dictated the messages.

Because I came close to dying from pneumonia at the age of four, my mother, as is maternally natural, concerned herself constantly with my health. Each morning I reluctantly downed cod-liver oil mixed with orange juice. Every school day from the Monday after Labor Day until the last day of school in May, Mother insisted I wear long underwear throughout my elementary school years. In those days no consideration was given to the threat of ill health to a child in heavy "long johns" sitting in an overheated classroom. The possibility of getting a chill from bitter Ohio winters worried Mother as much as my getting too little rest.

Her concern for my physical welfare must have carried over to the ethereal realm in which her spirit now dwells, for her second message to me read, "*You rest every day and let us do the best for you.*"

In going back over the first year of my automatic writing, I found the majority of Mother's messages contain some reference to my health or state of mind. "*Do not worry,*" she once wrote, "*for you will learn to know things soon. You will get help from all of us.*" Another early message from her suggested, "*Have no fear. You must be patient.*"

Mothers can be generous with praise and my mother, even in her ethereal state, is no exception. "*Every good thing will come to you,*" read one message she sent. "*You make much good happiness for us and also much for God. You help others and are good at many things. You are learning more each day and putting many good thoughts in your mind and soul. Do not worry for anything. We watch out for you and all you love. Be happy and know we do things for you. Love, Mother.*"

Once she sent word to me by way of a transcription signed by William. "*Mother says she is proud of you and sends always her love and good thoughts. You are to remember to be persistent as you were when you were a child, she says, and you will win all you wish for.*"

As the months went by, direct messages from Mother dwindled in number but became more explicit and longer. "*You must discipline your thoughts,*" she warned, "*and not let them wander to impossible lengths. It is part of the training—discipline—and you will gain much from it.*

"It is well to learn all you can, but trying to do too much at once, to accept too much at once can be confusing.

"Ondaras says to accept his word that all will go well if you let it flow and do not try to force anything. Relax and seek quiet. That is the best way to keep all channels to us open.

"We are here to help you put everything in its proper perspective. You will be of much good service to all who seek your aid. Do not worry. We are at your shoulder. Love, Mother."

Three months of sitting down each day to automatic writing passed before I heard from Mother again. The message was long and varied. *"Nothing,"* it began, *"is so important at this time as keeping your health to high standards. It clears the lines of communication and replenishes your energy. You must get rest and be ever watchful of diet and exercise.*

"We here are ready at all times to give you guidance whether it be for your writing or for your day-to-day growth of spirit.

"We are anxious to have the world know of us. Your conversations with others on this subject of spirit does much to keep thought waves going and they envelop others who will give much meditation to the subject and perhaps also join God's army. Every person you meet, indeed every human being on earth, is a soldier for God's army. But each person must listen to the clarion call—to be still and listen and he, too, will help spread the word to all mankind.

"You will plod onward with your writing and give as much time to it as you are able. Do not, however, put it off if it is at all possible. You must sift what at the moment is important and what is not. Anything of a minor nature can be put aside for another time."

Here Mother completely changed tack, calling attention to and commenting on people I know, which is rare among my Spirit Guides unless I ask a pointed question about a specific person. Once again maternal she warned my husband about his health.

"Ron is heading for more good work and he will know much happiness from his accomplishments. Tell him to be ever vigilant of his health to keep up his energy and his momentum so he can cover more ground easily."

Mother offered advice to a dear friend of mine whom I hadn't known when my mother was alive. *"Lorie is having a hard time of it. She has seen glimpses of the divine love she has had bestowed on her but how difficult it is for one to break off habits etched in for many years, and, too, an obstinate narrow mind makes for little absorption of truth."*

For another person very dear to me, Mother sent this message: *"Pat is gradually changing her thinking. One who has resisted change, yet has had it fall upon her at every turn—as in all of life, in all of nature. She is learning to bend with the wind without snapping. As circumstances change one must go with the flow or one is whipped by the treacherous current."*

As though wishing to include everything she had

missed for the past few months, Mother sent a parting assurance to end her long message. *"You will find what you are looking for. Never fear that we would let you flounder alone through life without our help. We are with you constantly and watch after your interests. We send always our blessings and joy. Love, Mother."* Whether here on earth or as guardian angels, mothers can be counted on to dispense wisdom.

Over the years of moving from place to place around the country, I have had many mailmen. None were so strange as William. A particularly moody young man, he seemed remote, quiet, and very withdrawn, seldom engaging in the usual banter that occurs between a housewife and the person who delivers the mail.

In those early days, being a suburban homemaker and mother, I considered the arrival of letters from a distant family and friends and the hometown newspaper the highlight of my day. I eagerly waited and watched for the mailman.

Blessed with an exceedingly outgoing personality and a love of talking, I bounced outside nearly every day, greeting William with a friendly smile and instant chatter. Never was there a hint of flirtation or personal interest in my demeanor, but I found his aloofness a fascinating challenge. As young as I was at the time, I thought his apparent discomfort at my verbal onslaught rather charming.

Only on one occasion did William step out of his

usual stoic character. I was dressing after finishing a shower; my two sons and a neighbor boy were playing on our front lawn. Standing in the bedroom in my underwear, trying to decide what to put on, I heard a terrible racket from the children—a fierce argument rapidly escalating into a full-fledged fight. Hurriedly donning the first housecoat I could find, I dashed outside to settle the disagreement and to check for any cuts, bruises, or black eyes.

Not until I returned to the house, the ruckus quieted, did I notice William dispensing our mail. Before I could say a word, he hissed at me like an irate father, "Don't you ever go outside in that housecoat again!"

Slamming shut the box he turned on his heel and loped quickly across the lawn, leaving me bewildered and wondering what could be wrong with my robe.

Indignantly I marched into the house, threw the mail on the bed, and examined myself in the full-length mirror. The robe was made of nylon, three layers of heavy nylon, as a matter of fact. Far from being décolletage, the garment buttoned to the neck, had a lace-trimmed collar and short sleeves. Instead of form-fitting it hung from the yoke like a wind-filled tent. How could such a demure garment cause so great an outburst? I walked away from the mirror and turned to look at the back. Vaguely, almost imperceptibly, the outline of my underwear showed through the material. I could not believe such a dim suggestion of a lady's underwear had caused William to lose his temper, but evidently it had.

Several months later we moved fifteen hundred miles away and I never saw William again, but in a letter two years later a former neighbor wrote, "By the way, you remember our postman, William, don't you? He was off our route for several weeks and I asked the substitute carrier about him. He told me William was seriously ill with a kidney ailment, then today he told me William died this week. I thought you might like to know because after you moved away William always asked about you when he brought a letter from you."

My astonishment at discovering through Lola that William, my Spirit Guide, was the same soul who had once been my mailman is quite understandable. The only time through the years I have thought of him is when I hear the song "Invitation." William heard the tune one day as I played it on my stereo when he was delivering the mail. Handing the mail to me he said, quite pleasantly, "You're playing my favorite song."

From the beginning of my automatic writing William assumed the role of spokesman for my small group of guides, signing the major portion of the messages. Dear William waxed more articulate in spirit than he ever did in his manifestation as a human being, urging me to learn more, to seek the truth, and to be patient.

Eventually I discovered the reason behind William's anger over the robe. During my early attempts at automatic writing I asked the guides to tell me when I lived in Japan, for I knew without a doubt I had lived there in at least one lifetime. The brief answer came in crude letters. *"Same as weeom."*

Unsure of the spelling of the last word I scrutinized it carefully. The *w* could possibly be interpreted as an *n* or *v* as could the final *m*. I asked the guides for clarification and they wrote, *"Wm."* Weeom certainly didn't look like William but my husband suggested I try pronouncing the word aloud in two syllables. *"Wee-om, wee-om,"* I intoned over and over. Finally I got it. The phonetic sound of weeom is similar to the pronunciation of William. William and I had lived at the same time in Japan centuries before.

"What was our relationship?" I asked of the guides. *"He father,"* came the reply. I laughed aloud. That explained the fierce paternal tone of my mailman when he told me, "Don't you ever go outside in that housecoat again!"

Ondaras and I, as Lola the psychic had informed me, had known each other in Europe when he was a street philosopher and I one of his followers. At one writing, I asked my band of angels if Ondaras and I had known each other in any other lifetime.

As though he were once again talking on a street corner, Ondaras did not hesitate, relating a remarkable account of our associations and his function as a master guide.

"Indeed," Ondaras wrote, *"yes, in very many centuries ago starting with your first near the beginning of life on this earth. In many manifestations I have been your teacher, sometimes in a school, often informally as a family friend asked to counsel a child.*

"Oh, yes, dear one, our paths have crossed many times on earth and many times on this plane where I now dwell forever. I have come back a hundred times a hundred or more, many more than you and for many centuries now I have ascended to master teacher and a member of the board. I shall not again manifest in human form for I have successfully graduated from my schooling to a place at God's side.

"My major function is to oversee several groups of God's angel guides. Several? Nay, hundreds are under my guidance but do not fear that you or any are ever neglected. With our high dimension frequency and vibration communication, I know in an unmeasurable instant what your needs are and I can give your angels or you immediate guidance.

"Oh, yes, we have known each other although when I was yet struggling on the path and you were a novice our association was not a pleasant nor easy one. Several times you failed to hear the guides calling, you turned your heart from God, you ignored all signals and suffered the

consequences—to return to earth and discharge your debt where often you succeeded and other times failed.

"However, I must add that the past several turns there you vindicated the previous errors and have, with each recent return, gained amazing insight. And this life now shows the most remarkable progress in the shortest time.

"I'm pleased to have a hand in your spiritual progression as your master guide. It has not always been an easy task with you in other lives but now you have crossed over the delicate line and the sword of knowledge has touched its mark. All ahead will not come easy. Do not think you have no work to do. You are yet a student, dear child, a good student but beware of becoming truant. You are a good student and a strong soul but the temptation will come. I have confidence, knowing you well, you will eventually conquer all and we here are ever at your side.

"You do well in your specific assignment and when this book is done, we will get on with the rest. Love, Ondaras."

Chapter 3

≈

In the introduction of this book I mention the dangers in automatic writing, indeed of any exploration into contacting the psyche or Universal Subconscious Mind. Incredibly perilous is experimentation by those individuals with the slightest trace of emotional or mental instability. Even those persons emotionally and mentally balanced can fall under the exhilarating spell of automatic writing and can jeopardize their health.

From the *Metaphysical Bible Dictionary* (Unity) comes this warning: "We should watch our emotional nature. We should not think that the spiritual uplift that comes to us, and the great demonstrations that we make through divine power are miraculous; if we do we are likely to be carried away with feeling and with appearances instead of remaining in conscious oneness with the Spirit of Truth, with the divine understanding. Stability and poise of soul must be cultivated, that we may not be unduly influenced by every wave of thought that seeps through our consciousness."

A particularly levelheaded career woman of my acquaintance who has been doing automatic writing for thirty years warned me repeatedly from the beginning of the hazardous aspects of the practice. "It can be all-encompassing," she cautioned. "Keep aware every day, every moment, for it can be mesmerizing."

I appreciated her concern, but I was convinced her words did not apply to me.

A woman I do not know but heard of through a mutual friend became so caught up in automatic writing she shut herself off from her family for several weeks, neglecting their emotional and physical needs as well as her own. Day after day she cloistered herself in the den, napping on a lounge chair when exhaustion overcame her, emerging from the room only to grab a bite to eat and tend to bodily functions. A threat of divorce forced her to give up the isolation, but not completely. She spends at least four or five hours a day secluded from her husband and children, hunched over her desk in the den absorbed in automatic writing.

The warning, of course, had nothing to do with me. Other people may be weak and uncontrolled, but not I.

Perhaps you have heard the tale about the farmer and his mule that was so stubborn the farmer was forced to tug, push, and pull in urging the animal to move, but to no avail; the critter wouldn't budge an inch. Finally the farmer thought of a solution. He whacked the mule smartly between the eyes with a 2 × 4 board.

A neighbor ambling down the road demanded an explanation of the farmer's strange behavior. "Well," drawled the farmer, once more cracking the beast with the board, "first you gotta get his attention."

To get my proper attention so I would be able to absorb their knowledge objectively without the intervention of my personal ego, my dear angels focused on the awareness of human passion. My guides cleverly saw to it that the first few messages from Mother and Van, either directly or through William, were flavored with the subtle condiments of their previous earth personalities. But without realizing it and through no fault of my angels, I soon became emotionally immersed in the writing.

Shortly after Daddy's identification of himself and his declaration of love for me, he sent this: *"Mother says you give much joy to God and to us all. Be of good heart and be patient. She sends love. Love, Van."* Tears blotted the paper and I could write no further that day.

Soon Mother herself wrote: *"Do not worry about anything. Have patience. I am proud of you. Be persistent as you always have been and you will win all you wish for.''*

I heard my mother's soft mellifluous voice whispering in my ear and I imagined her bright reassuring smile, a smile bestowed on me many times during my childhood. A flood of memories engulfed me and I wept, washing away the pent-up emotions of years gone by, the years when I had needed her wise counsel and knew only despair because she was gone from me, gone from the earth. Yet, here she was, she and Daddy, giving me sage advice. I experienced an exhilaration beyond description.

''You must rest some,'' Mother wrote one morning, *''and trust us to do the best for you.''*

Overlooking the fact that as a precocious child I received appropriate punishment from my parents for innumerable misdeeds, I enjoyed a continuous warm and loving relationship with both Mother and Daddy. To have them now touch me with their inimitable wisdom and humor caused me to fall into the very trap of which my friend had warned. Momentarily I forgot the day-to-day demands of my wordly existence.

For nearly forty-eight hours I neglected to plan meals, market, or do laundry. I seemed indifferent toward my patient husband. Feeling swept up in a cloud of vapor that lingered several feet above the living room floor, I drifted very near complete disassociation. Because I haughtily ignored any cautionary words, I became enveloped by a delusion of my own making. Personal ego can be a dangerous weapon against one's own well-being.

I have since read of documented cases of deep psychological problems, schizophrenia and, yes, permanent insanity resulting from attempts at automatic writing, use of the Ouija board, or other methods to reach the psyche. One must keep a balance.

Kundalini, a yoga discipline, aims for a point of balance between the conscious and subconscious minds. Without that balance one can become overly materialistic, aggressive or passive, uncaring and, yes, even mad.

One of the most attractive and outstanding cards of the tarot is Key 17, The Star. It depicts a maiden kneeling at the water's edge with one knee on the land and one foot in the water. One foot dips into the water of the subconscious but her weight is balanced and supported by one knee firmly planted on the earth (consciousness). In a reading of the tarot, if Key 17 is dealt straight up, it indicates great love given and received, insight, hope, and good health. If the card is dealt upside down, it signifies lack of perception, stubbornness, a chance of physical or mental illness.

In my studies I found a recurring factor being stressed. Balance. Perhaps in modern vernacular we could say it is moderation in all things.

In writing of his experimentation with brain waves

and hypnagogic images while in alpha state, U. S. Anderson, in his book, *The Greatest Power in the Universe*, states, "However far my imagination carried me, I knew I had an anchor in the physical world and it would not engulf me. That anchor was reason."

In the same book, Anderson points out that Nietzsche and van Gogh had fanatically plumbed the depths of the subconscious and both became insane.

Because I ignored warnings of the dangers of psychic exploration, my childish naïveté and supercilious vanity had led me into waters much too deep for one, all but rudderless, to safely navigate. The blame cannot and should not be placed on my loving angels. Just as the power to manifest good is in the mind of the individual, so is the power to create evil.

To again quote U. S. Anderson from another of his great books, *Three Magic Words*, "You are now experimenting with the greatest force in nature. We caution you not to become so wrapped up in it that you forget your daily life. Do not search for contact with the Subconscious Mind to the exclusion of the exercise of the Conscious Mind, for, as a human being, your goal must be to achieve a perfect balance between the great creative power of the Universal Subconscious Mind and the Conscious Mind."

Had I but read those words before I became so submerged in my experimentation, perhaps I would not have allowed myself to come to that nefarious state of euphoria. But then again, considering the inflated state of my personal ego at the time, I might have ignored the words as having nothing at all to do with me.

Fortunately for me my wise angels, under the sagacious direction of Ondaras, came to my rescue in a manner they knew would accomplish the same results as the farmer when he smacked the obstinate mule. By an abrupt change in the tone of the messages, my angels once again received my proper attention, but not before I swam about in a sea of confusion.

At an early morning session, shortly before dawn, I asked my angels about my sister who has experienced many devastating illnesses and tragedies. I particularly asked how I could be of help to her. Mother answered immediately.

"You cannot do for her what she must do for herself. She must now find help with the aid of the Holy Spirit and Self. She will be able to do this only if she wishes to know the truth."

I was stunned. Mother's attitude seemed unusually callous and distant considering my sister was also her daughter.

Then William offered, *"You must let Sister look for love and truth herself."*

Why was William speaking for my mother about her own daughters? And why did my father send the following terse message? *"Until you learn the real truth and learn to tell every truth from bad you will not be ready to go on and make the book to tell all the world of us."*

The shock I felt surged through my body like an electric current. I had presumed in the discarnate state he would not chastise me, yet here I was being scolded! Dropping the pen I studied the message carefully. It took very little imagination on my part to conjure up the stern tone of his voice, a sound I had heard many times in my life. He was telling me to mind my own business and not tell my sister how to handle her own spiritual growth. Of course! As obstinate as the farmer's mule, I had put aside the one premise prevalent in everything I had read on metaphysics and related subjects. Each man is responsible for himself, for his own soul, for his own conditions, for his own enlightenment, for his own discovery, growth, and salvation, his own balance. No one else can do it for him, not even God, until man searches within himself to find and use God's infinite love and power.

At that moment the sun burst gloriously over the mountains beyond my window, flooding the room with golden light. Just as suddenly I gained insight into my dilemma as though the sun's rays had penetrated my thick skull. My Spirit Guides were giving me a resounding whack to point out my error. I had allowed myself to personalize Van and Mother to the point of visualizing them as I had known them on this earth plane. I had become much more emotionally involved with the transmitters of the messages than the meaning of the messages themselves.

These discarnate souls which had once been in the earthly bodies of my mother and father had, in another lifetime, lived in different ethereal bodies that perhaps had not been acquainted with the mortal vehicle in which my soul was traveling at the time.

Mother and Daddy as I had known them on this earth plane do not send the messages. The wise words I receive are sent by astral souls in a higher dimension who once wore the outer covering which identified them as my parents in their last incarnation, but now they are my Spirit Guides, my guardian angels who call themselves Mother and Van.

That revelation accepted and its important lesson learned, I changed perspective, no longer looking at the writing as a captivating game, no longer viewing Mother and Van as the mortals they once were. I recognized automatic writing and the messages received as an important part of my climb up the pathway of spiritual growth.

That pertinent knowledge released me from the cloud of invisible vapor in which I had been living those two days and dropped me, as it were, with a thud on the floor of my living room with my understanding husband standing by. My wise teaching angels had presented a lesson designed to emphasize the role of my personal responsibility and control in attaining further spiritual progress, a progress that left no room for emotional imbalance.

Several weeks after Neven, a new guide, made his appearance into my writing, I received an urgent message, again on the subject of maintaining equilibrium in experimentation and communication in the spiritual realm.

"You would do well," Neven wrote, *"to inform those who read your words to be constantly aware of balance and harmony in their association with their subconscious, with God and with us. One can come into disharmony if he loses control and allows his carnal imagination to carry him to severe and dangerous depths. His psychological needs call him to misunderstand us and his association with us. He creates evil forces that sweep him along treacherous currents. It is possible he could be pulled under by the very forces he conjured up but used in error instead of good.*

"One must be aware that unless he keeps one foot touching and himself balanced, he will plunge into the abyss. All must be balanced, all must be in harmony or his testing our communication could bode him ill, a crisis of his own making. Properly balanced and harmonized one can attain giant leaps on spiritual growth.

"If one uses communication with us to his own selfish ends instead of the goal of spiritual enlightenment," Neven warned further, *"such a person shall find himself blocking the aisles of communication, defeating himself and the goal he had originally set for himself.*

"There are many beloved ones who established communication, grew in spirit yet allowed personal ego, personal vanity, and personal greed to overcome their lofty purpose. They shall reap what they sow and become diminished in capacity or else they will be made to deal with their mistakes after their transition and in future lives.

"Sound a warning then to all who would follow. Keep your soul balanced, your mind balanced, your body balanced and all will be in harmony. We send joy and blessings. Love, Neven"

Qualified legitimate psychics (overlooking obvious charlatans) who take the gift and dress it up "show-business" style and who charge fees are looked upon with disdain by many in the spiritual psychic community.

"It is evil," one very spiritual lady explained to me, "to charge a monetary fee, large or small, for use of the gift of spiritual communication. The gift is to give freely to help others when they ask. When anyone comes to you for advice through your automatic writing, you must do it willingly and for no charge to help others or else you will one day find the flow of communication is dwindling and you could lose the power until you once again find balance and harmony. Greed is evil and has no place in spiritual balance."

Among the dangers of psychic exploration, are there such entities as evil spirits in the discarnate that have the ability to "possess" a human being?

Although some automatic writers tell of abusive language, sexual innuendo, and malevolent ideas appearing in their writing, none has ever occurred in mine or in that of any of my personal acquaintances.

In asking God for protection prior to my writing sessions, I am attempting to shield myself from my own erroneous thoughts rather than defend against evil spirits.

In the strict metaphysical explanation as I understand it, evil occurs only when the subconscious conjures it forth. Ondaras stressed this premise when he answered my question concerning evil spirits existing on the ethereal plane.

"No, it is not possible," he announced emphatically. *"Many souls are difficult and impetuous on their first arrival here for they refuse to believe they have departed mortal life. Others sleep a deep sleep on a lower level because they have yet to awaken to their spiritual heritage and refuse to face the history of their souls. Others here are impatient to return (to the earth plane) before they should but all souls have the free will to decide and some learn to regret rash actions. But evil? No, they are but confused and always they are the young souls who have much to learn.*

"Have you not at some time in your life had a fear so great it seemed real and your imagination further amplified that fear into reality? Replace the word fear with evil and you see how a mortal may become 'possessed' by what he calls an evil spirit. It is created by the mind and fed

by error thoughts allowed to ferment in the subconscious. With this feeding, the thing becomes fetid, more rank, and swells to rotten manifestation. One does not need a special ritual nor a special person to rid himself of this scourge. It is in his own power to control himself and destroy the ugly thing he himself has created.

"No, my dear," Ondaras continued, "we may have souls here who are somewhat ignorant and retarded in their spiritual growth but they are not evil.

"Man must learn that if he is to refrain from calling up his imagined evil he must control his error thought. He alone is responsible. God is not, nor are the guides. Man has allowed himself to form an evil entity and has given it credence by recognizing it, labeling it, and passing control to it.

"Man must balance and harmonize himself with the vibrations of God and His Universe. When he accomplishes that task, his capabilities for manufacturing evil are destroyed.

"Balance, harmony, and love. Keep these in your heart and soul and there is no chance of evil danger. Love, Ondaras."

Yes, there are many dangers associated with delving into psychic phenomenon. The fault does not lie with God nor the guardian angels. The explanation can be placed squarely on the individual who has personal responsibility for the control of his own destiny, his spiritual enlightenment and growth, and who is also wholly responsible for control of his own emotions.

William, Van, Mother, and Ondaras, my spirit teachers, my guardian angels, as well as the new guide, Neven, presented me with a serious challenge. For finding answers as part of my schooling here on earth, I was charged with personal responsibility for it all. Would I be up to that challenge? My angels had appeared at the right time, in the right place for me and I could do nothing less than be open and receptive to their wisdom, their love, and learn who I am and why I am here on this plane. The journey and the lessons became more exciting as well as more challenging, and more of my angels awaited their turns to enter.

Chapter 4

⌒

For the first month or two after the onset of my automatic writing, the sessions continued to be very laborious. After a half an hour of sitting in quiet meditation with the pencil touching the paper, I considered myself fortunate to get three or four words, and often an hour's time was required to get any semblance of a sentence.

I was greatly elated when a twelve-word message, which had taken forty minutes to complete, came through from Van. *"You must work hard not make haste, you must move the world. Love, Van."* The abbreviated time factor signaled to me that the usual snail's pace of the writing was accelerating, ever so slightly, yes, but it showed a beginning, a sign of improving communication. I looked forward to each session with joyful anticipation.

All of a sudden, after about six weeks of daily

sessions of automatic writing, long before Neven came on the scene, various geometric shapes began appearing in the messages. Triangles, enclosed half-circles, figure eights listing at an angle, and full-bodied crosses. Some appeared in single file across the page in military-like succession while others jumped in, sometimes two or three at once, between the written words. Here is an example: *"Let the ◐ teach you the △, △ and you will learn ∞. You will learn † △ △ †. Love, William."*

Symbols abound in ancient literature, in the cabalistic mysticism of the Jews, in the many versions of the Bible, in the lore of the Gnostics, in the hieroglyphics of ancient Egypt, in the dogma of the Masonic Order, in literally hundreds of ancient esoteric documents. However, many months of research would be required to sift through endless numbers of religious and philosophical books in an attempt to find the answer to the mysterious figures appearing in my writing each day.

"Ondaras wants you to go to ◐ for this message," William directed one morning. *"You learn △ very soon. You must learn to be patient †."*

As a child I thrived on puzzles and coded numeric messages sent over the radio at the end of an episode of "Little Orphan Annie." Of course, I sent in the required number of Ovaltine box tops to get my coveted secret decoder ring. As the announcer recited the numbers I wrote them down then consulted the precious magic ring for the corresponding letters of the alphabet and solved the puzzle: ANNIE LOST, an ominous message hinting at the next day's adventure.

My guardian angels allowed me no such facility for solving their coded messages nor did they offer much in the way of a clue as to what lay ahead. *"Learn to seek ☽ and you will move the world." "Learn you well ☽ and find 8 ✝." "Look for △ and love the enemy."*

Totally baffled, I watched each day as the symbols became more prevalent. On several occasions only triangles appeared in various positions—resting on a side, standing on a point, or leaning at a precarious angle.

"What do the symbols mean?" I asked of my Spirit Guides.

"You learn △ soon," was William's response.

Because the profusion of symbols rendered the writing exceedingly dull, each day I pressed the angels for an explanation. The answers themselves became equally tiresome. *"You learn more love and truth and soon you know." "Soon you know more love and truth then you learn more." "Let more love and truth come into your mind and soul."*

Since explicit information was not forthcoming, evidently I was on my own. I would have to do something for myself without any definite direction from my guides. They pushed me headlong into the vast ocean of mystery but, very wisely, not without a life preserver of sorts. The Bible was the first floatation device the guides tossed to me.

"Read the Book of Knowledge," they wrote.

"Which Book of Knowledge?" I asked.

"The Bible," they responded.

When I asked where I should start in the Bible, William, with a rather tongue-in-cheek tone, retorted dryly, *"At front."*

Every day I pored over the ancient tone, starting "at front" as I had been instructed. The Good News version offered easier comprehension and very slowly truth began to sink into my brain. In reading Proverbs over and over, I realized I was not the holier-than-thou person I had imagined. All my life I had tried to be kind, helpful, thoughtful, loving, cheerful, prayerful, and all the other attributes I had been taught to exercise. But I was prone to gossip with the neighbors; intermittently I allowed a hot quick temper to flare; I sometimes became depressed with a what's-the-use attitude; now and then I neglected my prayers and my attention to God was not properly focused. My angels pinpointed these errors and demanded I do something about them.

During my daily plodding through the Bible, I asked for help from the guides who, after a few days of ignoring my plea, suggested I read the Book of Revelations. My prior attitude in reading that final book of the Bible had been one of frightful confusion. John's horrendous dreams and visions impressed me as being wild unexplainable nightmares, the kind experienced when one has eaten something spicy before bedtime. This particular reading, however, was performed with the knowledge, as stated in the Good News version, that the visions of John are presented in symbolic language, which would have been understood by the Christians at that time in history, but would have remained a mystery to all others. So, the Book of Revelations is a coded message.

Revelations 1:3 reads: "Happy is the one who reads this book and happy are those who listen to the words of this prophetic message and obey what is written in this book! For the time is near when all these things will happen."

Thus I read Revelations from beginning to end on orders from my Spirit Guides. However much I learned, nothing explained the symbols the guides were drawing haphazardly on my paper. Stars, lamp stands, swords, horses, living creatures with eyes front and back, seals, scrolls, scales, trumpets—none of the above appeared in my writing. Rather impatiently I asked once again for the guides to enlighten me on the meaning of the symbols coming through the automatic writing. An extended dissertation followed.

"Read again the Book of Revelations. Check it with the taro[t] cards and learn what it says to you. We will help you know what the symbols mean and you will learn much

of all things. Be of good heart, be patient and knowledge will come to you. Love, Mother."

Tarot cards? How strange! At this point I had never seen a deck of the cards much less had any idea of what the game is about or how it is played. Weren't tarot cards used by Gypsies and fortune-tellers? How could they tell me anything?

I called a second acquaintance who had been doing automatic writing for more than twenty years. Without revealing the message about the tarot cards, I asked, "Do you have any idea what all those symbols in my writing mean?"

"Have your guides not told you?" she questioned.

I sighed. "No, they just tell me I'll learn soon."

"Hmmm," she pondered, "they really want you to work hard on your own, don't they? They have a reason for not telling you directly, never doubt that."

"The writing is getting so boring," I told her, "because of these figures which keep cropping up."

"I would suggest," she said firmly, "you find a book on the history and explanation of tarot cards. Perhaps it will shed light on the symbols they are sending."

After hanging up the phone I whirled to face my husband. "Can you believe it?" I cried excitedly. "She suggested tarot cards just as my angels did!"

My husband was as astonished as I but even more so when the phone rang a few minutes later and a newfound friend called to say, "I'm going to stop by with some books for you including a good history of tarot cards and also a large deck of the cards. I think you'll find them interesting."

The coincidence was almost too much to believe. My dear angels were helping after all, making sure all of these study aids were strewn in my path where I could not help but stumble over them.

The Rider Pack of the tarot consists of seventy-eight cards; fifty-six of which are called the Minor Arcana with the cards evenly divided into four suits—Wands, Cups, Swords, and Pentacles. The remaining twenty-two cards make up the Major Arcana, which depicts human figures and symbols in various experiences or situations.

The first card of the Rider Pack is Key O, The Fool, so-called because he represents the naive, ignorant, inexperienced soul about to step into earthly manifestation. He carries over his shoulder the wand of will. Tied to its end, hobo-style, is a bag said to carry universal memory and instinct. Another interpretation of the bag, the meaning of which seemed to apply most closely to my case, is that it holds four magic symbols The Fool will have to define and learn to use during his trek through life's cycle. The picture on the card shows The Fool standing on a spiritual elevation about to step over the edge into physical manifestation.

Although there are several versions of the tarot cards and a profusion of theories concerning the interpretation thereof, any one of them contributes greatly to an understanding of esoteric wisdom. Based on ancient philosophies and religions, the tarot symbolically traces the soul (The Fool or Joker) from its entrance into earth manifestation through a journey of human experience where it must press onward through life forced to choose between good and evil. This basic explanation will have to suffice in this instance although the study of the entire deck of tarot is more complex and much more illuminating.

How did all this apply to my writing and the symbols I had been getting? According to the tarot, a triangle (pyramid face) suggests the threefold principle of wisdom, love, and power, or elementally light, heat, and energy. The Bible offers the Divine Trinity of Father, Son, and Holy Spirit while metaphysically these three correspond to mind, idea, and expression or, if you will, thinker, thought, and action. In man the triangle is spirit, soul, and body, the triumviral basis of holistic healing.

The figure eight, whether slanting or horizontal, is, in the tarot, the cosmic lemniscate, a symbol of eternal life and dominion of the spiritual over the material. The figure further indicates the harmonious balance sought between the conscious and the subconscious. The figure eight has no beginning and no end, signifying the eternal life of the soul.

The enclosed half circle indicates a cup. Imagine, if you will, a wineglass with the stem broken off. The bowl in one dimension suggests a half circle. In tarot the cup is associated with divine knowledge or, as in my writing, can be interpreted as the Book of Knowledge. A cup holds the water of cosmic knowledge which can be stirred to action by meditation and prayer. The cup of consciousness of eternal life. Love, pleasure, and enjoyment are also read into the cup symbol of the tarot cards.

The type of cross coming through my writing was a full-bodied solar cross with equal arms, the type seen in several cards of the tarot. According to the tarot it indicates union with God and earth and is the solar symbol of the balance of forces. Also the upright bar (the positive element) merges with the horizontal bar (the negative element) to accomplish harmony and balance.

In metaphysics the cross signifies the crystallization of the inner current of divine life (perpendicular bar) with the cross current of the mind of the flesh (horizontal bar). The cross in any definition conveys divine blessing.

The search for the meaning of the symbols with which my Spirit Guides bombarded me had directed me to a fascinating in-depth study of the tarot, its ancient history and the significance of each card as applied to the entire deck. That knowledge led me to understand more fully the reason for my being; why I am on earth and what I must do to make life's journey a successful learning experience. I suggest a study of the tarot if you wish to further expand your knowledge and comprehension of the divine relationship between you and God, the Finite and the Infinite.

My teachers, the Spirit Guides, put me through a very tough curriculum in this grade level of school, but once my mind absorbed the meaning of the symbols and the true meaning of life everlasting, the geometric shapes never again have appeared in the messages. Ondaras, William, Van, and Mother had hit their target and received my proper attention for all time.

Shortly after putting aside the tarot, having studied the subject five hours or more a day for several weeks, I received this laudatory transmission from my angels:

"You make much good work learning of these things. We are much glad you dig so deep to find the truth and to know all things. You please God and each of us who love you. Ondaras says you did very well but you have much more to learn every day. Keep to your mind and soul. We are glad for your path to light, for your journey up the mountain, and we are much glad we finally got through to you. Go now and learn more so you can tell the world of us."

Chapter 5

~

Documented cases of guardian angels' influence by way of automatic writing go back at least as far as 1870 when a reputable English clergyman, who also served as a schoolmaster, tuned his subconscious to such a fine degree he could read a book at the same time a message from his angels was being written.

A Spanish nun, highly respected in her community, received the writing while in such a deep trance she remembered nothing of having written a word.

For twenty years, beginning in 1919, an American woman, admitted she "heard a voice" while writing more than twenty volumes on esoteric subjects. These books are known as the *Patience Worth* series.

Down through the ages the existence of Spirit Guides in the discarnate and their influence on people, cultures, and religions have been recognized by human beings of enlightened minds over the entire globe. Many authors, far more capable than I, have written of communication with discarnate spirits. Why was I so chosen and ordered? Why, then, with millions of words written about angel guides, did mine insist I *"tell the world of us"*?

When I put the question to the guides, they gave no exact reason while cleverly skirting the direct question. *"You must do no more work,"* William ordered, evidently referring to my part-time job, *"then when you learn more of love and truth you will make a book to tell the world of us."* Nearly every day there appeared some mention of the book I was to write to let the world know of them.

Impatient as usual and perplexed as to a precise literary formula, I once again asked when I should start the book and how it should be structured. William replied, *"You will know when you are ready. Do not worry that you are confused as to what to write or how. Ondaras says when the time is right you will know."* I decided if my dear angels had all that confidence in me, then I could do no less for them.

From what the guides had told me, I saw the need to prepare myself in every possible way to be fully qualified when their signal came. I picked up the long-forgotten daily habit of writing—articles, letters, stories, poems, and dissertations on social concerns. The somewhat rusty writing techniques needed oil. I resigned my job devoting several hours a day to meditation, prayer, intense study, and concentrated writing.

The correct decision must have been made for William soon wrote, *"Ondaras says you are doing much good. You learn more each day and put much of that learning into making a book. We send our love and blessings. Do not worry for anything for we watch over you. We are much pleased that you can tell the world when you have made the book."*

Three months into automatic writing the script changed to that of a sixth-grader. The letters were neatly formed, rendering the messages much more legible. The words came at a faster pace although *t*'s were not yet crossed nor *i*'s dotted. One sentence still ran into the next, yet I cannot remember my childhood handwriting as being so orderly.

With fascination I watched the writing evolve. I held the pen, yet the script was so unlike mine. Also, while writing the messages I had a vague awareness of what I was transcribing but in rereading the copy it seemed as though I had never seen the words before. The messages astounded me. They still do as I read them over.

Although the guides never let up on their insistence I write the book, they became more philosophical and offered expert advice, especially in the area of concern for my son who was going through a period of depression and great personal conflict following a divorce from a woman whom he loved very much.

"You will show son the way," the angels advised, *"and he will see the light of truth. He has very great potential in this life. Deep inside his soul he wants to follow the path of truth but he does not recognize this fact. He has free will to decide for himself. If he chooses the wrong way to go, he will find much sorrow and he will lose joy and much success. He must listen to you now or he has lost the game."*

I found it gratifying, to say the least, that the guides did not tell me to mind my own business as they had with my sister. They encouraged me to help my son. *"Son is confident he knows best how to play the game of life,"* they continued, *"but he should know he plays only with or against himself and no one else. He must play with great care if he is to know joy and all he dreams of. Otherwise, he could lose it all. You must tell him so and hold him all around with love. If he understands, his mind and heart will heed. Lift him up like a small child who stumbles, but do not sicken yourself with worry. Help him to see, but let him choose."*

The next day, William wrote, *"Tell son he has much great good ahead in this life if he will but listen and see the great light of wisdom. He will not make his goal in this life if he does not listen to the soul inside. We will help him if he asks and looks deep for us. Do not take his burden on your own soul but love him. Wrap him all around with rays of love and light."*

The son in question is a very sensitive soul who is quite familiar with the subject of reincarnation. He thinks me neither kooky nor flipped out for my tenacious belief in the metaphysical and reincarnation; thus, when I showed him the messages from the guides, with no personal comment from me as to what I thought he should do, he did not reject their advice, nor did he instantly accept. In a loving and poignant letter a week or so later, he told me he was aware and working on his path up the mountain. Could one ask for more? Far from telling the whole world, I had at least reached one other person. Perhaps he would have the opportunity to help yet another. Though not exactly spreading the word throughout mankind, I felt the guides had taught me a valuable lesson. Even though the book seemed but a distant manifestation, I could daily put into practice the guides' wise teaching. The opportunities for just such measures arrived in droves.

A friend of thirty years whom I had seen only five times in the past two and a half decades arrived for an extended visit. During all the time of our acquaintance we had never touched on the subjects of God, Spirit Guides, reincarnation, or the like. Although we belonged to the same church and sat side-by-side in the alto section of the choir, our association involved social functions, the activities of a local theater group, and the bookings for a trio we organized. This left us little time to deepen our friendship with metaphysical or religious discussions. Though family moves parted us, we kept in contact several times a year.

As my husband and I awaited the arrival of Evelyn's plane at the Los Angeles airport, we debated the best approach to take in confronting her. After all, metaphysical tomes graced every available shelf space in our apartment. Mounds of typing paper and manuscripts surrounded my desk and typewriter, for I intended to continue my daily communication with my angels.

How would Evelyn react to this evidence? Her husband is a scientist and she a biologist as well as an archaeologist. Perhaps she would totally refute our ideas as bizarre and judge us inappropriate hosts, and catch the next plane home.

My husband and I agreed to drift toward the subject gradually, testing her reaction before going on to the next idea. Knowing Evelyn's extremely witting side as well as her intellectual acumen, I felt she would rise to the occasion with grace and good humor whether or not she found our beliefs strange.

Amid welcome hugs and kisses and compliments, I heard a little voice in my head tell me it was all right and I relaxed a bit. By this time I had learned to acknowledge any type of communication from my angels be it a muted voice in my head or through the writing.

Our plans called for dinner in Marina del Rey to

avoid the evening traffic rush and to give us some time to think over our approach. Impatiently, I posed the question just as we drove away from the airport.

"Have you heard of automatic writing?" I asked from the backseat.

Half turning in her seat on the passenger side, Evelyn responded with a rather sharp "What?" Had she not heard my question? Was she surprised that I knew of automatic writing or was she totally unaware of the practice?

"Automatic writing," I repeated, "have you heard of it?"

My husband looked frightfully uncomfortable, as though silently telling me this was neither the time nor the place for any such revelations. Perhaps I should have waited until we were well into our dinner, relaxed and loose.

"Good heavens!" Evelyn replied with some amusement. "A woman I know has been doing it for quite a few years and spends several hours a day at it. Don't tell me you are into it too! Well, good, maybe I can get some answers to some things I've been wondering about. My friend doesn't give readings. Shall we ask your angels when we get home?"

With a great deal of relief the three of us went on to enjoy a delicious meal and most interesting conversation. Later that evening, when sitting across my dining room table from Evelyn, I became somewhat apprehensive. Never having given a reading for anyone except my husband, I explained to Evelyn I only write what I "hear," that I have no way of knowing whether the information is fact or fantasy, but that so far "the kids" had been very helpful with their advice. She understood and asked if she and I had ever lived in another lifetime together.

The pen moved swiftly as the guide dictated a strange story. *"Yes, you were sisters and you were very close. You lived in South America and you had a pretty home. You did happy things in Brazil where your father made ships. Your name, Elena; she, Rosalita. Then you went away to a far place in the north to make a new home with your husband and you never see her more. Rosalita never went away but stayed to die of aloneness. You died having two small children. Do not ask more of this now."*

Evelyn look at me solemnly. "Perhaps that explains," she offered softly, "why I have felt so close to you through the years even though we live far apart."

I nodded. "I'm sure of it," I replied, "but isn't it strange they demand I ask no more?"

"Well, maybe they know the memory of it might be too painful for you," she suggested.

"There is something else unusual." I went on, "For some inexplicable reason I have always had a strange aversion to Latin music whether it is South American, Mexican, or Spanish. Of course, Segovia is an exception. It is odd but I have never been able to explain why I am fascinated by Spanish architecture and even the language, but the music hurts my ears and makes me nervous. I wonder if there is something unpleasant in a past life in which Latin music played a part?"

"Well, you won't find out right away because they definitely wrote 'Do not ask more of this now.' "

I agreed and turned to the task of answering her next question. "I would like to know," she said, "if Martin Smith is there. He—"

I interrupted. I told Evelyn I preferred knowing nothing more about the gentleman because I was concerned the information might sway my personal consciousness and I might write what I thought Evelyn would want to hear. I was not yet confident about personal readings. I wrote the name Martin Smith on the paper and silently offered my prayer for guidance and protection.

"He is very happy here and learns more for his next time," William wrote. *"He says it is not as hard here as he thought it would be and says never fear."*

As I relayed the message Evelyn's eyes widened and I knew the guide's words had struck a chord.

"I'm sure glad to hear that," Evelyn said with apparent relief. "Martin died of cancer and was quite fearful of his impending death. Your message puts my mind at ease. Thank the kids for me."

Subsequent questions brought equally satisfying answers to Evelyn. Once again, through my Spirit Guides I was able to help someone. For a moment I toyed with the thought that my lot in life might be in psychic readings through the writing. I asked the guides. William answered immediately. *"Your big goal is first the book but when someone wants to get a message from us do not turn them away. Help them when they ask, for we all must do what we can to spread the truth and light of God."*

Well, that was that. The book. My guides had an obsession with the book; I had no idea when to start it nor did I have a specific outline in mind. But the die was cast. I would write the book. This time I truly believed I would write the book.

A few days after Evelyn flew back to Texas, I sat at my desk thinking through the subject and outline of the book. Suddenly, a title popped into my head. *Spirit Guides: Angels in the Army of God.* During the next day's session of automatic writing, the guides, through William, dictated nearly a page of chitchat.

"You are on your way and it must feel good to you to finally have direction set. We gave you the title. How do you like it? Be assured we know it will catch the eye of those who are curious about us. You will do well to continue in this vein until you get the material you need for your second book. All things will be accelerating for you. Keep faith burning brightly in your heart and soul and do not waver from the path. God is pleased, Ondaras is pleased, and we here are as joyful as children at recess."

Here I paused for I had a clear vision of my dear

guides rolling about in heavenly stardust, perhaps even sliding down the Milky Way in their joy.

"You have opened your soul to God the Creator," William continued, *"in all you do, in all you see, and in all you think. Keep these things in your heart at all times and feed on them for they are manna to the soul just as food to your belly."*

I thought it extremely crude the angels used the word *belly* instead of stomach but I learned early on to never try to predict how the guides will word their messages. The writing went on: *"God's food will nurture you in all ways. Never lose sight of your goal for one instant and it will grow within you and get bigger and easier to attain. We look forward to working with you each day with much joy and pleasure. Love, William."*

With such devout encouragement I could not let the angels nor myself down. I was ready and eager to tell the world of them. So I sat at my keyboard and began writing.

Chapter 6

☞

My first husband and I, plus our two children, lived in Texas from 1950 to 1958, the year my husband's company transferred him to its headquarters in Philadelphia, a move I did not want to make, for many reasons. I loved Houston and had made many dear friends there, including Evelyn.

Never being too keen on snow and cold weather, even as a child growing up in Oak Hill, Ohio, I didn't want to leave tropical Houston and move to cold, dreary, snowy, wet Philadelphia. But, of course, as the dutiful wife and mother, I had to make it seem like an exciting adventure to my children to ease their transition to a new home and school.

Privately, I wept oceans of tears. How would I ever cope? Would I be able to handle all the traumas of the move as it affected my sons? The transfer was a big promotion for my husband. He had worked very hard for it and deserved it. Naturally, I would not make the move difficult for him by voicing my reluctance.

A few days before the time to leave, I stood at the kitchen sink, crying, as I looked out at my lovely neighborhood. I clung tenaciously to the wonderful memories of the good times and loving friends. I DON'T WANT TO MOVE! I wailed loudly to no one but myself.

A silent but firm voice in my mind interrupted my sadness. "You will meet someone very important in your life."

Thinking the thought came from the positive, cheery side of myself, I replied aloud, "Oh, yeah? Who? Man, woman, child? Who?"

The evenly modulated voice sounded in my head once more. "You will meet someone very important in your life." Every time I wallowed in my sadness, the same voice, the same message, stopped my tears.

The day of the move arrived much too soon for me. My husband stayed behind to tie up business at the office while the boys and I took the train to Ohio where we were to stay with my parents until a rental was found in Pennsylvania.

I remember very well the date my sons and I left Houston: January 18, 1958. As we waved frantically from the moving train to a disappearing daddy, my eyes filled with tears. I could not, would not, cry in front of the boys. Then I heard the voice again: "You will meet someone very important in your life."

I smiled broadly at my sons with the sad faces. "Well, guys, we're off on a wonderful adventure!"

Eight years passed before I met that someone the voice had predicted would be important in my life. Even then, I didn't recognize him, not until three years later. The path to the revelation of the man as the *someone* predicted by the voice I now know as that of one of my angels, hopped, skipped, and jumped through my ordinary life, across a span of many years. Now I will telescope those years by hopping, skipping, and jumping to the highlights.

It actually began in 1951 when we bought a house in a new neighborhood in Houston. One of my neighbors was a charming woman by the name of Margaret Kallina. On meeting her, I commented on her name. I had never heard it before and asked the origin. She told me it is Czechoslovakian, a name alien to one reared in a Welsh settlement in southern Ohio.

Cut now to 1959. Driving down the Main Line from our new home in Paoli, Pennsylvania, I saw a sign outside a restaurant advertising the entertainment as Ronnie Kalina at the piano. I wrote to Margaret inquiring as to the difference in spelling of the name. Someone at Ellis Island, when her husband's ancestors arrived in America, she explained, added the extra letter.

Only in retrospect have I been able to significantly connect the vignettes. My angels' plans were perfectly timed to allow me to mature gradually.

Seven years later, in April of 1966, I became a fashion model for a department store. In August of that year I modeled in a show next door to a restaurant where, later, all of the models stopped in to relax. At the piano was a man named Ronnie Kalina. Once again I wrote to Margaret to report the event, still not recognizing the angels' scheming in the series of coincidences. My husband was transferred to northern Ohio in 1967. We separated two months after arriving and I moved back to Pennsylvania, and resumed my former modeling job. We were soon divorced.

Can you see my angels' plan for all of this? I didn't; not for one moment did I even suspect they were guiding me. I hadn't forgotten the voice that said I would meet someone very important in my life, but I had met so many people who qualified I was no longer interested in finding anyone in particular.

My angels had already selected this person. He and I were married in 1971. It was then that Ron (I never did call him Ronnie) told me of an angel whispering in his ear in 1968. I had walked into the restaurant where his jazz trio was playing. As I appeared, he heard a voice say, "There might be someone for you." Startled he turned to his bass player who was so absorbed in the music he couldn't have said it. Again the voice spoke to him as I found a table. "There might be someone for you," his angels said.

We have been married more than twenty-four wonderful years, with each year becoming more loving and precious. I can attest that angels certainly know what they are doing in guiding one's life.

"You will meet someone very important in your life."

How right they were!

Chapter 7

Spirit Guides, eternally helpful, routinely send warning signals of impending problems. That a mortal fails to react to the signs in no way deters the ever vigilant guides from relentlessly repeating the warning. If the mortal were alert to the clues and followed through with appropriate action, much expense, time, and hassle could be eliminated. In the event a person does not heed the alarm and finds himself in a troublesome dilemma, the guides do their utmost to help find an ultimate solution to the human-caused predicament. In December 1975 Ron and I moved to sunny southern California.

My husband and I received many indications our car needed attention. Profuse oil and water loss told of evident leaks somewhere. "We must take the car to the garage," we told each other, yet neither made a move to make the necessary arrangements. Instead we checked the oil and water each time we used the car and added any elements necessary.

One sunny afternoon while driving on one of California's miraculous freeways to a routine appointment with the chiropractor, I noticed wisps of smoke racing past my window. Sure that the car zooming past me was the culprit, I maintained a steady pace of fifty-five miles per hour. Just as I approached an exit several miles from the one I intended to use, a familiar muted voice said, *"This one—NOW!"*

Stubbornly I refused to get off the freeway in strange territory. The exit a few yards ahead was not the one I intended to take. At that moment a big cloud of steam poured from under the hood of my car. Suddenly I found myself coasting down an unfamiliar ramp with a dead engine. At the foot of the ramp, I jumped from the car at the same instant a pedestrian ran across the street to help. A young man in the car behind turned on his flashers, directing exiting freeway traffic around me.

The Good Samaritan lifted the hood. Rusty water bubbled from the radiator as the acrid stench of burning oil seared our nostrils. Totally distraught, I wailed to the stranger, "I'm going to be late for an appointment!"

He smiled. "You're lucky, lady. There's a gas station with a service bay on the other side of the freeway underpass."

I screamed loudly. "That isn't going to get me to

my appointment! How will I get the car there? My husband has to go to work tonight; this is the only car we have. I'm in a strange neighborhood. How will I get home? I—"

Inside my head a loud voice said, *"Keep calm. Take one step at a time. Hysterics will not solve the problem."*

Without attempting to identify the commanding Spirit Guide or argue with it, I accepted the order for I knew the voice was right. I found a nearby phone booth, called the Automobile Club for a tow, then called the doctor to postpone my appointment. Next I phoned my husband outlining my plans, and asked him to call my son for the loan of his car in case we needed it. If the car could be repaired while I waited, I would drive home. Otherwise, if it had to be left at the garage, I would take the bus.

The car, incapacitated with a malfunctioning thermostat, a broken carburetor, and an assortment of minor ailments, had to be left in the strange garage in the hands of an unfamiliar mechanic. To add to my frustration, I learned my son could not be reached. I used the long ride home to analyze the inconvenience that had happened to me.

My Spirit Guides had done their best to warn us of impending trouble. Neither my husband nor I had paid close attention. Our busy schedules precluded obeying the well-intentioned angels. Yet they saw to it the Good Samaritan was near at hand and the young man was behind me to direct traffic. Had the accident occurred at any of the exits beyond, a garage would have been nearly impossible to find so near the freeway for it was less residential, more open country. The guides had given me as much aid as possible.

Two days later my son drove us to pick up our car. As we pulled away from the garage, nearly $300 poorer, the engine sputtered, coughed, and died. We turned back to the station. After a half hour of waiting for the mechanic to make an adjustment, we were once again on our way.

My first reaction, typically Aries, was to angrily retrace our path and give the mechanic a violent tongue lashing while demanding he do the job perfectly. *"No,"* the angel voice in my head ordered, *"take it to a place closer to home."* We decided to do just that. No telling how many days we would dicker with the mechanic. We could not afford to waste the time.

Mistakenly, we forgot the guide's warning. Daily concerns demanded our attention and we neglected car maintenance, despite having to add water and oil to the car before each use.

A few weeks later my dear angels issued further warnings about our negligence. En route to work one night my husband found himself in the middle of a freeway traffic jam with a stalled engine. He prayed to God and pleaded with the Spirit Guides for help. Immediately the car started and Ron drove to work.

The same night, returning from work at three a.m., the car stalled at the foot of a freeway exit ramp. The Automobile Club came to the rescue.

With all these signals from my angels, it is difficult to understand why we did not take the ailing car to a trusted nearby mechanic the very next day. Busy with our separate schedules, we put it off.

The ultimate tragedy occurred the night the car broke down as my husband was on his way to a job thirty miles away, with all his equipment and a fellow musician in the car. I borrowed a car into which we transferred the musicians and their equipment and raced to the job, leaving the car to be towed.

If we had only acted on the signals from the concerned Spirit Guides, we could have avoided paying an additional $658 for car repairs and $250 for a rental car for two weeks.

Utilizing their precognitive powers, the Spirit Guides had previously taken precise steps to lift much of the financial burden from our shoulders. The week before our car's demise, the two owners of our apartment complex fired the manager, walked to our apartment, dumped an armload of papers, keys, and log books on our living room floor, and declared, "We want you to manage this building."

Coveting our privacy and anonymity, we refused, only to discover they were persuasive and formidable in argument. Finally, they asked, "Would you take the job until we find someone else or you decide to take it?"

The urgent voice of one of my angels whispered, "Yes."

I found myself parroting the unsummoned guide. "Yes," I said aloud. "We'll be the managers." Ron and I struck a suitable financial arrangement with the owners. As managers we paid no rent, and within three months or so we were able to recoup our debts.

Several days later Ondaras wrote, *"We are aware of every circumstance. Utilize every encounter as an opportunity to learn for it becomes rather a baptism of fire, so to speak. Make the most of every situation and you will know what it means to grow. As long as you are aware of any probable error on your part you can use that knowledge to your good advantage.*

"Be always trusting that we are here to help you. Do not worry for money for it will be taken care of. Trust us to supply you with all you need. You are not to worry for the why or wherefore of anything at all for it will come to you in due time."

Ondaras was right. When the final car repair bill came due we had already saved that amount from not having to pay rent. The Spirit Guides must have anticipated our stupidity in ignoring their warnings and provided us with the wherewithal to pay our debt without drawing on our savings. I judge them shrewd financial advisers.

Among the guides' perpetual talents is the ability to perform as excellent detectives. Any lost article can be found almost immediately if one just asks the angels and trusts that they will find the missing object.

Ron became particularly perturbed one evening when he could not find a certain sheet of music. "Will you please ask your friends"—he pleaded in exasperation—"where that music is? I had it this afternoon and put it in this notebook, but it's gone—lost!"

I put the question to the guides. William replied, *"He has not lost it. He will find it when he gets a message to us on his own. Then he will find the song."*

As I read the message to Ron he immediately made a silent request that the music be found. An instant later he got up from the piano, walked over to a little-used storage cabinet, and chose one of the many books on the shelf. "If the music I'm looking for is in here, it will be a miracle. When I asked the guides, this is where they told me to look."

Ron opened the book and inside was the missing sheet of music. "I don't remember having put this in here!" he exclaimed.

When looking for misplaced objects, a calm resigned attitude speeds the process. Frantically racing around the house looking in every drawer, under every book and cushion causes emotional frustration which in turn tends to block communication with the angels. One must assume a peaceful attitude, visualizing the object and establishing solid faith it will be found. When I first discovered the guides' detecting ability, I went so far as to present a rather lengthy formal plea explicitly describing the lost object and stating where I remembered seeing it last. Now all I need say is "Okay, kids, where is it?"

I am led to the object at once. If the item in question is not in the apartment, silence eminates from the guides. Then begins a spiritual version of the question–answer game. "In a pocket?" *"No."* "Under the couch?" *"No."* "In the car?" *"Yes."*

Finding anything left behind in a public place becomes more difficult, but not impossible. However, concerning an item that might be stolen, the answer is likely to be: *"It is of no consequence. Learn from your mistakes."*

Guardian angels are amazingly efficient teachers.

Chapter 8

A man in his early thirties, from one of the movie studios, who arrived for his first appointment exactly on time, seemed rather embarrassed. Donald (not his real name) fidgeted during the preliminary explanations of automatic writing. I asked that he not give me details, only a name and what he would like to know.

Gulping audibly, he said, "I'd like to know what relationship Pete and I might have had in another lifetime." (Pete's name is also an alias.)

Having previously uttered my prayer for protection before he came in, I began writing, barely paying attention to the meaning of any words being written. As I wrote *Indian Ocean*, I remember thinking I hadn't thought of that place since sixth-grade geography class, and continued taking the angel's dictation. When I finished writing, I read Donald a fascinating story.

"You and Pete were sailors working on different ships plying the Indian Ocean. Ashore, when you met in the village pubs, you more than likely fought with each other, for tension seemed to grow between you."

A wisp of breath escaped his lips. I looked up to see his eyes opened wide. He looked at me in awe. I continued reading.

"On one occasion you found you were shipmates and tried to steer clear of each other, but when a raging storm came up, and the captain was found overcome with strong drink, you and Pete joined together to lead the men and save the ship.

"From then on, although you never became close friends and tension sometimes rose between you, never was there ever again hate or fighting."

When I looked at Donald, his face had paled quite visibly. "Does this mean anything to you?" I asked.

He nodded, unable to speak for a moment. Then he began a very interesting story. "Pete is my twin brother," he explained, "and we have had some fairly rough times liking each other. Recently, he returned from living in a small village on the shores of the Indian Ocean. He said he had been curious about the place for many years and finally decided to spend a year there. When he got home, he said he had found some peace but no answers. This reading explains a lot."

Donald said his good-byes and thanked me profusely. I reveled in the surprise of it all and was very pleased that the angels seemed to have helped him.

I didn't hear from him again until two months later. He called to tell me he had talked to his mother in another state just that day and told her about the reading.

He was astounded when his mother asked if he remembered when he and Pete were in seventh grade, and their English teacher asked her students to write a fictional story. She gave permission for Donald and Pete to write one together. The twins wrote about two sailors saving a ship in the Indian Ocean when the captain was drunk.

Donald thanked me for the reading and told me he and Pete were getting along a lot better than in the past. The reading helped him understand.

Laughing in delight, I thanked the angels for showing me once more how the readings helped others and for allowing me to be the conduit for their transmissions.

Chapter 9

⌒

According to my erudite Spirit Guides, part of my duty here on earth is to heed the requests of those who wish to be helped through readings by way of automatic writing.

My experiments with the private consultations for my son, husband, and friend Evelyn, had been interesting and enlightening but what could I do for strangers who might be recommended for a reading? I soon found out.

A friend who is a member of a women's group associated with radio and television production asked me to give readings at a club-sponsored conference for college students majoring in media communications. In addition to exhibits and workshops, the program would include a tarot reader, a card reader, and me. Since the October meeting had been planned around a Halloween theme, the committee felt it would add "fortune-teller" atmosphere to have the various readings.

Reluctant to have my angels' communication labeled "voodoo," "occult," or "magic," I declined her first invitation. In addition, the thought of giving two- or three-minute readings to a succession of young people, perhaps as many as twenty or thirty in a three-hour period, caused great apprehension. Amid the noise and questions, how could I enjoy the tranquil meditation and prayer I deemed necessary for proper spiritual contact?

For several days I prayed on the matter, asking God and my guides whether I should accept the invitation. Then, at the end of a long philosophical treatise from William on keeping to my goal of spiritual growth, came this answer: *"Help any you can when you get the opportunity."*

I accepted my friend's invitation to appear at the conference, nevertheless voicing my doubts as to my ability to read for strangers. An automatic writer herself, my friend could understand my apprehension but added, "It's about time you dived into a situation like this and got your feet wet. You'll enjoy it."

Enjoy it I did, though I was not prepared for the consuming interest and the confidence in me shown by most of the people who crowded into the tiny room I was assigned.

Before leaving home that afternoon I spent a half hour in concentrated meditation and prayer, requesting that I be given blanket coverage for the entire afternoon's readings. Meditation and prayer would have been impractical before each of the nearly forty readings I gave that lovely day.

Two bright-faced young ladies first sat before me. One asked if I could give any information on a previous life she may have had. As I wrote her name and age at the top of the paper, I gave a quick silent plea to my angels to come to my rescue as soon as possible, and they obliged.

"You lived in Japan and the friend who is close to you was your sister," the guide wrote. *"You shared many confidences and good times of laughter. You married brothers and lived side-by-side where your children played together. You have always been helpful to each other in every life."*

When I read the message the girls turned to each other and giggled. Finally, one said, "We think you should know that although we look Occidental we both are half Japanese. Neither of us has ever been to Japan—in this life, that is—but we have this longing to visit there sometime."

"Have you known each other long," I asked, "or are you related to each other?"

They shook their heads. "We just met about a year ago," one of the girls replied, "but it is as though we've known each other all our lives." Smiling broadly she added, "I guess you could say many lives, and we are a big help to each other."

As they rose to leave they thanked me and walked away together chatting gaily.

A shy beautiful girl with clear tawny skin next sat before me. She glanced at me then dropped her eyes.

"What is your name and what is your question?" I asked.

Her voice, nearly inaudible, was soft as a kitten's purr. She told me her name and said she didn't have a particular question, could she just ask the guides for any advice they wished to give.

As I wrote in silence, her hands rested on her lap. When the writing stopped, I picked up the paper, watching her face as I read aloud: *"This child has marvelous potential in many areas, particularly the arts. She is well suited for writing and has much talent in this direction. She must, however, have faith in her spiritual beliefs and faith in her ability. The wellspring is full to overflowing and she will do great things."*

As she looked up, her eyes widened, full of wonder. A slight smile touched the corner of her mouth. "They told you all that?" she asked in a near whisper. I nodded. "How would they know," she continued, "I have always wanted to be a writer since I was a little kid?" Not waiting for an answer, she went on in a strong firm voice. "Everybody laughs about it, even my family, but now I know I'm going to do everything I can be a writer." Clutching the paper, she thanked me, walking away with a purposeful stride.

The young man facing me next was tall with dark hair and charmingly crooked teeth. If I were but thirty years younger, I thought, he would be the type for me—a sincere smile, a masculine bearing but with an aura of gentleness.

"I'd like to know about some other time I might have lived, er, that is, the soul that's now in me," he stammered shyly.

I listened carefully as my Spirit Guide dictated: *"He lived in the North, in Alaska, where he braved very bitter cold to hunt for food for his large family. Many times he was frightened by wild animals which attacked him and which he had to fight off sometimes with few weapons. Although he was frightened there was much courage there. He must learn that to be frightened does not indicate one has no courage. He can learn an important lesson from this for this life. Do not be ashamed of fright when you have courage and faith."*

I glanced at what had been written and before reading the message aloud, I asked, "What do you know about Alaska?"

He seemed to jump to attention in his seat. "Alaska?" he repeated. "I've read *Nanook of the North* more times than I can count."

After hearing the message he leaned toward me and whispered confidentially, "I sometimes get scared."

Taking the paper I offered, he commented, "I don't

99

know how this stuff works but it sure came at the right time. I can't thank you enough.''

As his lanky Gary Cooper-like frame sauntered away, he quickly turned and smiled. If I were twenty again, I would make a point of seeing more of that young man.

Not all readings that day were joyful. An older woman, apparently pursuing a college career while in her forties, sat in the chair with a thud, loudly announcing, ''I don't believe all this crap, you know.''

''Well, that's your prerogative,'' I replied, smiling while fighting down the argumentative nature of my personal ego. ''You aren't interested in a reading, then?''

A chorus of voices behind her urged her on. ''Go on, Pat, what have you got to lose? Have a reading!''

''Oh, all right,'' she said, turning to me, ''but I'm not going to ask about past lives because I don't believe in reincarnation. Just tell me anything.''

Silently apologizing to my angels for her doubt, I leaned over the paper. *''One must be still and listen to the voice of God within himself,''* Ondaras wrote. *''Each person is a part of God and God is a part of each person. Do not think that what you know in the material world is all there is to life and all there is to the universe. God is everywhere yet God is in you. Listen and heed the voice you hear.''*

When I finished reading the woman asked, "Do you mean to tell me we are all little gods?"

I shook my head. "No, you misunderstand. You must—"

Grabbing the paper from my hand, she croaked, "This is a bunch of hogwash. I'm glad I didn't have to pay for this. I don't believe a word of it."

Turning to her friends she cried, "Let's get out of here," stuffing the paper in her handbag. "It's all a bunch of trash. I'm wasting my time here."

When she cleaned out her purse, did she throw away the paper or instead reflect on the words of the angels and perhaps see a glimmer of God's light?

The predominant question that day concerned past lives. Curiosity about past lives, where one might have lived in the centuries past, stirs us all, but the reward comes when one utilizes the information of other incarnations to recognize past errors and learn from the lessons offered. Communication with one's angels should not be viewed as a titillating game, but as a valuable learning tool toward spiritual growth.

Spirit Guides have access to Akashic records which, of course, are not written down as we record things but are deposited in the spiritual "memory bank," or, as Ruth Montgomery refers to it—God's heavenly computer. In the fourth dimension, communication is mainly by thought—instantaneous thought waves provide instantaneous thought answers, a premise difficult for us humans to comprehend with our sense intellect. In the same way, spirits communicate with mortals—by thought waves. Paul Foster Case, in his book, *The Tarot*, explains the method this way: "Knowledge of the higher aspects of reality comes to us through soundless sounds of an Inner Voice which often speaks as plainly as any voice heard with the physical ear. The reason is that the hearing centers in the brain are stimulated by higher rates of vibration, which serve as means of communication between ourselves and more advanced thinkers."

Questioning Spirit Guides about close relatives who have recently departed can often relieve guilt feelings and assuage fears.

One of the women who timidly approached my desk that exciting and fulfilling afternoon said quietly, "I would like to know about my mother who is dead. She died a few months ago."

Despite the firmness of her jaw and the set stiffness of her lips, I detected a sadness in her eyes. It seemed the entire experience pained her, even the reading.

I inquired of the mother's name, no more.

"She is very happy here," the angel wrote, *"happier than she ever knew possible. She says she wants you to know that now that she is here she better understands about many things there."*

I looked up from reading to see tears quivering on the woman's lower lashes ready to spill over. "The message means nothing to me," I offered softly. "I have no explanation or interpretation as to what it means but perhaps you'll know."

She nodded vigorously, spilling a tear or two into her lap. "Yes, yes, I do," she answered breathlessly. "It means a great deal to me and I'm grateful to you. Thank you." Gently folding the paper she placed it tenderly against her heart as she left.

A few days later William sent a kindly message: *"Perhaps you are now persuaded that you can use this to help others. Did you not feel the vibrations flow? You gave much help to all and they will think on these things many hours."*

Chapter 10

The experience with the people at the Women in Television Conference gave me the confidence to agree to do a reading for a close friend. Judy especially wanted to ask about the child of a dear friend of hers whom I had met on several occasions. I was aware the child had been confined to a wheelchair for most of her twelve years and was in and out of hospitals throughout her short life. Yet her courage had been a constant source of inspiration to her parents. I had never seen the child nor did I ever ask Judy any particulars about her illness. I did not learn of her passing until several months later.

One of Judy's first questions was about the child. When she attempted to explain further, I asked that she tell me no more for fear my mortal mind would sway my subconscious with any more information.

A strange thing happened at the moment I started

writing. I had a faint vision of green rolling hills, a gurgling stream, a lush forest, and the sound of laughter—a remarkable occurrence that had never happened before.

"She says to tell you that she is happy here tending to all the children and running with them across the fields. It is beautiful here, she says, and the sparkling fresh air delights her. Have no fear for she says she runs and the air is so clear and beautiful."

Tears sparkled in Judy's eyes as I read to her. "You know," she remarked, "that dear child never walked, and now she's running."

"All I've ever known about her, Judy," I replied, "is that she was confined to a wheelchair and that her mother and you, too, gave her tender, loving care."

"You mean you didn't know the other trouble?" Judy's eyebrows shot up in surprise.

"Other trouble?" I shook my head. "No, I just knew she was crippled, perhaps deformed from birth."

"Oh, no," Judy cried, "that loving child had a debilitating muscular disease and for years it affected the muscles of her lungs. It was scary when she couldn't breathe . . . she would have to be under oxygen and each breath we thought was her last. So many times I heard her cry, 'If I could just breathe!' During those spells she had to fight so hard to breathe." Judy smiled wistfully. "I'm so happy she mentioned the sparkling fresh air. I'll tell her mother she's happy, she's running, and she's breathing clear air. It will do so much to console her."

Judy then asked if I could give her some information about the deceased adult son of an older friend of hers. The man had passed on only the year before. I warned Judy to give me no more information, not the slightest hint about the man, only his name.

One of my loving angels began at once and I could hardly believe what I was hearing with my inner ear and seeing being written on the page before me. When the writing stopped, I laughed, telling Judy I had never had a message quite like this one. I added that the man must have had a bubbling personality.

"Oh, yes, he did," Judy replied with excitement. "To the very end he joked and told us not to worry even though he was riddled with cancer and in terrible pain. What does the message say?"

I read from the paper. *"His first words on arriving here were 'Wow! This is great,'"* the guide wrote.

Judy clapped her hands in delight. "That sounds exactly like Jim. He always said 'wow' about everything he liked."

"He basks in the joy here to a great degree," I continued. *"He is forever joyful."*

Judy's beautiful blue eyes brimmed with tears. "Could I ask a special favor of you? Would you consider giving a reading for his mother? It would comfort her so. He was very special to her."

I agreed. Had not my angels ordered me to help those who come to me? They have told me I am to help when and where I can. There was no doubt that, so far, people were helped considerably by the readings from those heavenly, loving advisers . . . my angels.

Several days later Jim's mother, Mrs. K, came to my home for a reading. She brought a gift, she said, because Judy had told her, *I did not ask payment for dispensing God's gift.*

The beautifully wrapped package contained a sorely needed leather loose-leaf binder and a half-dozen ball-point pens, each pen printed with the word SPIRIT. On the first page of the notebook, the clever Mrs. K had written: "Write on—and on—and on!"

Mrs. K's first questions naturally dealt with her son, and a reliable angel came through with assuring words which satisfied her immensely. Her final question was, "I would like to know what to do about Robert."

When the transcription began I had to stop writing. I couldn't believe what I was hearing. I asked the question again, but the answer repeated. My guide, usually austere, philosophical, and divine, seemed completely out of character in the writing.

On seeing the hesitation in the writing and my obvious puzzled expression, Mrs. K inquired as to the trouble.

"I can't write this," I said.

"Why not?" she questioned, rightfully perplexed.

"Because it's a bit raucous. I've never received a message like this from the guides, not from any of them."

With a twinkle of amusement in her eyes, the lovely Mrs. K said, "If it's raucous, it's from Jim. He was quite outspoken, straight from the shoulder. He pulled no punches. What did he say about Robert?"

With some embarrassment I read, *"Jim says to kick his butt out."*

Mrs. K's roar of laughter shook my chandelier. "That is just about the way Jim would put it!"

When I asked the identity of the hapless Robert, Mrs. K told me he was an employee of the store she had jointly owned with Jim. Since Jim passed on she had trouble conveying to Robert she is now in charge and the only boss. Further, Robert had become incompetent in his work. Whether to fire him had been a constant worry, since Jim had hired him.

"You seem to have your answer," I told her.

"Yes," she answered brightly, "but I'd better fire him in a more genteel way than Jim suggested."

Before leaving my house, Mrs. K gave me a most precious parting gift—a warm embrace and a kiss on the cheek. "I hope you know the enormous comfort you and your angels have provided me. Thank you so much."

Not all discarnate souls are so pleasantly ensconced in "heaven" as the majority of spirits my guides had written about. When I questioned the state of the soul of a friend's departed mother, William countered with, *"She is on a lower plane and will rise when ready."*

"Why is she on a lower plane?" I asked.

"She must learn love and look to God," William responded. *"She must learn to love the world."*

In earthly manifestation, I discovered, the woman had been somewhat meddlesome and quarrelsome. She had delighted in orchestrating other people's lives to the extent she caused discord among friends and relatives, and near-divorce among married couples of her acquaintance. Her possessive attitude toward her son resulted in the dissolution of his marriage and contributed to grave psychological problems which plagued him for many years.

Presumably, the woman had learned very little in this life. Her soul was not prepared to face the truth when it departed the body and arrived on a higher plane. Thus, by her own subconscious choosing, her soul is in limbo on a lower plane until such time as it stirs enough to awaken to God and love. Her soul has many years of further schooling ahead.

Several months later I inquired about the woman again. Ondaras wrote: *"She has more time to spend in learning before she rises higher. Many times the education process of that type takes eons in earth terms. It could take much time, more than you realize. With the prayer and help from those on earth, she will rise sooner. Do not forget her in your prayers."*

We, then, can help discarnate souls just as they can help us. We can give thanks to them and pray that they, too, continue in their spiritual growth. Whether here or there all souls are a part of God with the same objective—to grow in spirit so as to one day be at one with God the Creator.

The angels have taught me so much in many areas of learning, but none so gratifying as the ability and opportunity to help others with the spiritual wisdom dispensed through the guides. It is at those times I am encouraged more than ever to tell the world about them, to spread the word that God's disciples, angels in the army of God, are waiting expectantly to help each of us when we call.

Chapter 11

My first indication of a "changing of the guard" within my little group of guides came through a two-page communiqué concerning my apparent spiritual growth. The angels assured me that much more was in store for me in the days ahead.

"Some of us may go on to help others," the message concluded, *"but Ondaras says he is ever watchful that you get only the best advice and instruction for you have made successfully the many steps he knew you could take. It came in good time. We send love and blessings. Love, William, Van, Mother, and Ondaras."*

Since others tell of different guides appearing in their automatic writing, I had fully expected to encounter additional spirits sometime in the months and years ahead, but I did not foresee the possibility of any angel actually parting company from my group. This was startling news: *"Some of us may go on . . ."*

I felt a great deal of apprehension. Which of the guides would leave me? Would it be Mother, who watches over my health and protects me when I travel? Or perhaps Van, the spirit of my father who always, carnate or discarnate, has been a strong influence in my life? Surely William would not go away. He seemed to be the head teacher under Ondaras and the designated guide to lead me on the path.

The message was clear; at least one of my guides would depart. Who would appear to take its place? Naturally, I felt a tinge of sadness that one of my dear guides would no longer appear. It would be like saying good-bye to a loving and trusted friend. Why must any of the angels leave?

The answer came at the next day's session. *"I, William, will be with you only a while longer to help. Do not fear that I would leave without warning and preparation and also do not fear that any change will come about in your instruction and guidance. On the contrary. My purpose was to prove to you without a doubt that we are indeed here poised to help. Otherwise you might have deemed us but a joyful wish without fully believing, but with my surprise appearance there would be no doubt in your mind. Ondaras says he, of course, will constantly oversee your schooling and the others who come will advance you in less time.*

"This is as it should be for the plan of a soul's advancement. I shall look in from time to time because I am look-

ing with much pride on your accomplishments. Never despair, never worry; only love and learn. Love, William.''

William had communicated his last direct message. Although I looked forward with curiosity to a new guide, I was reluctant to bid William good-bye. Ondaras himself appeared in the writing the next day with further explanation of William's departure.

"The pattern of things is changing. Be aware of this so you can better swing with the tide. You will be getting soon more information and with greater speed than before, in much volume, so you can use more now that we have your concentrated attention.

"Be not alarmed over the changing of the guard here. It is natural, a part of the scheme of things. William will return now and then. He has done his work well with much love for he says you always were a special soul to him. He is pleased you were able to learn so quickly your lessons.

"Keep to your path for others are ready to give you the lessons you need as you progress. God is pleased with William and his work. He must go now to more important matters which need his attention.''

I let my mind wander back to the day Lola, the psychic, confirmed my old mailman, William, as the main spokesman for my guides. After the initial shock and disbelief at his appearance, I had come to look forward to his advice and almost daily visits. No matter how strong Ondaras's assurance, I admit to a certain uneasiness at William's disappearance.

The next day Van sent a message of encouragement. *"The new era is nearly upon us,"* he wrote, *"and you will learn much you need to know. The writing of the books should continue and they will come about much faster in the days to come.*

"Do not concern yourself with the future except how it affects your learning and growth. Each day on this earth is precious to enjoy, to appreciate, learn and grow. You can do much to spread the word. We are ever watchful over your activities and send much blessings to you. Love, Van."

Some time had passed since I had heard directly from Van, the soul of my father; it was even longer since Mother had communicated directly. The succeeding message, maternally wise and supportive, came from her.

"You must discipline your thoughts," she wrote, *"and not let them wander to impossible lengths. It is part of the training, discipline. You will gain much from it. Learn all you can, but trying to do too much at once, to accept too much at once, can be confusing.*

"Ondaras says to accept his word that all will go well if you let it flow and do not try to force anything. Relax, that is the best way to keep all lines open. We are here gathering to help you and put everything in its proper perspective.

"You must not concern yourself with William's transition for it is natural and the change is always quite expected, although we know, of course, one hates to see old

*friends leave. Do not worry. We are at your shoulder to
help and whisper in your ear. Love, Mother."*

I felt better. In the nature of things, William moved
on when his work assignment was finished. He had
said he would look in from time to time. I had leaned
heavily on William's advice, even though the other
angels also dispensed excellent advice. Perhaps I de-
pended on William emotionally. Without emotional
support, would I be able to accept the guides' words
as readily? Would I be up to what they asked of me?

Van, naturally reading my thoughts, wrote, *"You
will be able to go ahead much faster. We know you sometimes are very doubtful if the road you take is the one you
should. We know you wonder if you are capable of what
we ask of you. Let us assure you the answer is yes, you
can and you will.*

*"Do not expect to sit down and get it done just like
that. It will not happen that way. You must work, rest,
work, rest. It is the best way to attack the problem and
get yourself balanced and in harmony, so never despair
that you are doing nothing.*

*"We here are pleased with your progress and as soon
as the new one gets acclimated, you will note a surge in
your production. We want the work to go well for it will
let the people of the world know more of us. Love, Van."*

The next day, as the first words of the writing
flowed across the page, I sensed I was being introduced to my new Spirit Guide. Perhaps to the casual
reader its words would seem no different than the

others I have received, but I, by now finely tuned to their wavelength, knew, without a doubt, this was William's replacement.

"Tell the world we wait for each and all the people of the world to open to us so we may help them," the message began. *"They need not be in such despondency, in such unhappiness if they would but see the light. They are more concerned with themselves, their mortal selves, than with the everlasting souls they truly are. We stand by waiting and eager to come to the aid of each man, woman, and child.*

"Look to God and you will find us for we are His Disciples ever doing His bidding. Look to God and you people of the world will at last know joy, which you seek now in the wrong ways, in the wrong places at this time.

"First open your eyes, open your hearts, open your souls so truth and light and love may enter therein. Do away with the trash of yourself you do not need. You are mistaken if you think the trash is important to you. Admit your errors. Conquer personal ego. Stand in the ray of God's light. Awaken! Love, [signature]*"*

I could not make out the signature because it looked like some sort of shorthand phrase. My husband, who had no better luck than I deciphering the name, suggested I ask for a clarification, which I did promptly. This time I could make out the first two letters as possibly *ne*. The next letter would have been an *r* or a badly executed *x* or *v*. The last two letters of the name were clearly *en*.

So this new guide of mine was *Ne_en*, something or other. I put this question to my angel. "I am unclear as to the spelling of your name. Could you clarify, please?"

That a Spiritual Guide could become impatient is inconceivable; nevertheless, by the tone of the answer to my question and the fact it came from Ondaras instead of my new guide, it seems my insistence annoyed the master teacher. He replied immediately: *"It is of no consequence at this time. You will learn when the time is right. Your new guide is replacing William for a time and will give you sage advice. You will do well to obey in all things."*

I felt like a child who had been properly scolded for an innocent refraction, but I could see no harm in wishing to know the name of my new guide. Ondaras did not let me pout for long.

"Van and Mother are here yet to see to their jobs," he continued, *"but it is Ne_en [the spelling no clearer] who will direct you most frequently. You will continue as you have with the words you write and all will come together eventually. Don't worry for it will be done.*

"We are pleased that you are so diligent and that you believe in all truths presented to you. Keep on the path and reap the glory of it all. Love, Ondaras."

The appeasement from my master guide salved my wounded ego and I turned my attention to the daily sessions with what's-his-name who wrote in articulate, fluent fashion. I knew he would be of great help for he gave no-nonsense advice, not only to me and for me, but concerning others as well.

In doing a reading for a woman, I was asked about a friend of hers I do not know. The new guide counseled eloquently: *"She is a much confused child and has looked no further than her eye can see for answers. Her debts are her own; no one pays for them for her. She must learn the lessons of life if she is to grow in the light.*

"She must cease mourning for it does no good but only riles up emotions better left undisturbed. The energies expended for naught should be put to more constructive use. The ultimate aid is love and prayer, love and prayer.

"Oh, if we could but make that understood to the world, our goals would be more easily met. One must not interfere with another's lessons for to do so is to deny him the opportunity to seek his own way with the help of God. One can, however, love and pray. Love, Ne_en."

After the reading I was informed the woman in question is facing a prison term for a narcotics violation and my friend wished to help.

As I read my new guide's philosophical treatise I was reminded of a question I put to an acquaintance who does automatic writing. I asked if her angels ever dispensed philosophical advice. I can hear her delightful laugh now. "Ye Gods!" she bubbled. "I sometimes feel as though I'm working in a Chinese fortune cookie factory."

My new guide, whatever his name, in the middle

of a week's worth of expounding, exhorting, and advising, sent this message:

"William will be looking in now and then so you need not fear he is lost to you. You understand, of course, his major assignment with you is finished and it is well done. Both of you worked exceedingly well. Therefore, he must go on his path as you must continue on yours. Love, Ne_en."

By this time I referred to my new angel as Neven, which seemed the closest interpretation of the signature. Since he voiced no objection, Neven is the name I used. Soon my curiosity got the better of me again, and I asked two questions at once. "Who is Neven? Am I spelling the name correctly?" A gentle reproach came forth. *"In due course you will learn. It is of little consequence at this time. You have come as close as is possible at this time. It is better you accept for now and you will be guided to that knowledge at a later time."* So I dropped the question . . . temporarily.

I sincerely missed William but could not deny the powerful lessons being taught by Neven. In addition, his transmissions were fast and clear. I could barely keep up with his dictation. Often I asked for a short break to rest my aching arm. Neven was very obliging, but once we started again, the words came even faster.

After several weeks of writing for a half hour daily, I was told by Neven I need only think of what I wished to know or ask and the angels would be in my mind and heart in an instant. With this encouragement, I dared once more to ask, "Who is Neven?"

There was no evasion in the reply. *"You have known me many lives ago but not in recent times. I was your master teacher even then when we were both mortal and you were an apt pupil. Together we studied much of life and the stars and much of philosophy which your eager mind absorbed like a sponge. You were but a boy then but very wise for your years. There were other times, many times when the paths of our souls crossed. So you see I am come to replace William for a while since he must now see further to his own growth. He did well in attracting your attention which was the reason he came to you almost the instant he arrived here but you did not notice at the time.*

"You have made great strides in just a short time and shall go even further in a short time. We want you to tell all mankind of us, so you must once again get in full harmony and balance. Now, go forward with no like questions on your mind. Love, Neven."

When well into the writing of this book, I received from Neven several pages of information on the reason for my being told to write the book, for he, too, stressed repeatedly the motive behind their urging me to tell the world.

"The world will be a better place, a Utopia, as it were," Neven began, *"if each person would but see to his own soul, to his own spiritual enlightenment. There is* [sic] *so much evil forces in your world created by those who turn*

away from God seeking their own worldly pleasures to the detriment and harm of others. Those who do thus will pay dearly for their deeds.

"Your task is to touch as many souls as possible urging each to look deeply in toward to touch God so they can avail themselves of the abundant power which is theirs to use. The task seems formidable, does it not? Your writing will touch many who may be able to see the light and they in turn will touch others who might not take the access to your writing."

I presume, by not taking access to my writing, he meant those who read this book would tell others, for others might not be likely to browse in a bookstore or frequent a library where it could be found.

"It is imperative," Neven continued, *"that as many souls as possible there on earth know of us and get in contact with us so we can guide them directly to expedite their development. Each person in the army of God, who uses his own talents for the purpose of instructing others, makes an incalculable contribution to spreading the word of us. As God's disciples, we can do much more good when more people know of us and call on us for help.*

"Many others use their particular talent in their own way to broadcast news of us. You have been chosen to write of us and, by your type of writing, teach, convince, persuade others to join the ranks. Some will preach, some will teach, some will even sing and act out their praise and thanksgiving in acknowledgment of God and the Christ. We who are the disciples, who are the teachers,

guide and direct those mortals who bring their appeal before us.

"You will carry on your writing under our direction and when this book is done, we will guide you to the right place in which to submit it. Those persons will be understanding of your writing and will help you in all possible avenues of aid. We send joy and blessings. Love, Neven."

Smiling to myself I noted my loving angels were now literary agents. Well, why not? God and my Spirit Guides coauthored this book. They were detectives and financial advisers. Why not literary agents? Anything is possible through God, the Creator. All the guides ask in payment as agents is belief, love, and action.

Chapter 12

❧

My first venture into offering questions to my guides concerning world events came in early November 1980, shortly after pictures beamed from the spaceship flying near Saturn were shown to the world.

"Today Voyager I flies close to Saturn. Do you have a comment?" not even guessing what sort of answer would be forthcoming. Neven dictated this reply: *"We, of course, know and watch all things. The leaders in charge of the earth-to-space project will be even more confused when the final analysis is compiled. Some scientists will shed their restricted thinking; others will fail to comprehend the significance of the evidence. It is a moment of great magnitude, for man is ever closer to unearthing the truth and those of us here are excited at the prospect of more humans expanding their minds to include us. It will help immeasurably with our projects."*

Several months later, scientists involved in processing data sent back over a billion miles of space from Voyager I confronted startling paradoxes and confusing mysteries when reviewing information gleaned from the space probe. Admittedly, even the veteran scientists were at a loss to explain the spectacular incongruities in many phases of the discoveries. Somewhere, I believe, highly advanced minds know the answers.

Global affairs are not usually a priority concern of mine when sitting down to contact the angels, thus I ask few questions in that area. Ritually, after a five-minute meditation to get myself balanced, centered, and quiet, I give a short prayer asking for God's guidance then I state, "I am open and receptive to your guidance with loving thanks." I let the guides take it from there wherever they wish to lead.

However, in early February 1981, I asked a specific question of the guides. Should the United States take a more aggressive position in space exploration? Neven immediately responded with a most interesting answer. *"Yes, and she is far deeper in planning than is aired to the public. In addition to important scientific data to be garnered, there is much to be learned about fourth dimensional travel, thought transference, and the like. Scientists, many at least, must have things proven to them in black and white on a grid in terms they can accept with their five senses and their mortal intellect. Can man plan love; can man explain the soul in completely scientific terms?*

"You recall the baffling rings of Saturn? We could very easily explain those but our word would not be acceptable to man's limited thinking."

Knowing Neven's transcription style very well by this time, I was aware that he was suggesting some very exciting and startling information will be awaiting us, perhaps not so far in the future as we might think.

Neven's words brought UFO's to mind. I have never seen one, but have often wished the opportunity would present itself. I have no doubt that some who claim to have had an experience with extraterrestrial vehicles are not lying; they have seen an unidentified flying object. Twenty years ago I did not believe that possible. I deemed the encounters as purely hallucinatory, but in studying metaphysics, self-realization, reincarnation, yoga, psychology, religion, and ancient mysticism I have found the idea entirely possible.

I refrained from asking Neven if the fluctuating black spaces in Saturn's rings were caused by space vehicles which might be invisible to the camera. I made no silent comment nor did I question Neven further. I merely allowed the writing to flow on.

"The mind, the consciousness, the unconscious, the subconscious," Neven went on, *"must be expanded in all directions, far beyond the limits man now thinks of as the*

ultra outer perimeter of his mind. Why does man put himself in a small rigid container, tell himself what he sees within the tiny box is all there is in the world, in the entire universe? Of course, from his narrow and limited viewpoint, the tiny cell in which he has closed himself is all there is to his life.

"If he would expand his consciousness, his awareness, cast off the fetters binding his mind, he could rise to a higher dimension of thought and learn the secret of life, the secret of the universe.

"Man must change; dissolve his rigidity, rid himself of selfish vanity, and turn to God who will allow him to discover his true soul."

Here Neven offered truly exciting information. *"We in other dimensions fill the galaxies. We communicate with each other and some on earth instantaneously. Higher souls, keep in mind, have a more expansive view and are not chained, not imprisoned by a small mind nor by human senses. Stand on the ground and look around you. Now climb to a spot above and look down. You see more from an elevated spot, do you not, than from ground zero? Because of our spiritual growth and expansive evolvement and being able to control the subconscious, we travel from dimension to dimension in a millionth of a second.*

"Yes, we are everywhere and those on earth who open their minds will one day see us. The world will be changed when we are at last recognized. Blessings be on you. Love, Neven."

My mind does not have a scientific bent, but I could easily understand Neven's point. As I have learned over and over, anything is possible. The loving angels, from their "expansive viewpoint" (an understatement if there ever was one) are aware of everything going on in the universe in an instant.

On November 6, 1980, two days after Ronald Reagan won the U.S. presidential election, Van sent a political message which I had not solicited by even a fleeting thought. *"The country in which you live,"* he wrote, *"will see renewed joy and many will come up from the depths they have mired themselves in.* (Daddy always had trouble with sentence structure.) *Hope now springs eternal and shall recognize the glory of living with God in the heart. The days ahead will be difficult but faith and action will win out."*

On reading the part about renewed joy in our country, I laughed. I vividly recalled the years of my childhood when Daddy, a staunch Midwestern conservative, would rant and rave, stomping about the house waving his arms, shouting, "Those damned 'Bull-she-vicks' and damned liberals will soon rule the world and ruin us all!" Conservatism had embedded itself deeply into his eternal soul.

More than a month later, in late December 1980, a warning for America came in the writing in a mini-essay. *"The country is, as you know, in great danger and until all turn to Spirit with the proper attitude much trouble could ensue. Your new president could do well.*

One must be sincere of heart and mind and know the truth. He must heed the inner voice and see with the inner eye. Vanity is his biggest stumbling block.

"He is sincere and could do well to get the nation back on the route it was intended to take. Everything leads back to the individual, who is the person responsible. We urge all to return to the basic principles on which the nation was founded.

"Each soul is responsible for himself and should see back to the root of all, which is Spirit. Never give up hope, for the army of God, of which we and you are a part, is continuously working for the betterment of mankind through Spirit. Love, Neven."

Shortly after the American hostages were released from captivity in Iran, Neven commented, *"The world will one day know peace if each human being would search deep in his soul to discover union with God. Some of those just returning have advanced rapidly in their spiritual growth for they were isolated from what they took for granted and were forced to turn inward to find themselves.*

"It was a trial; a severe trial. A few did not like what they found there; a few others turned away from themselves and dared not look further. Some will join the army of God for they saw how shallow is the word of those who profess God but act contrary to Spiritual Law, all the while proclaiming the deed is done in the name of God.

"Histrionics, theatrics all directed by emotion and not by the hand of God. This those returning learned and will heed well. Love, Neven."

One week to the day after I received the preceding message, a newspaper article quoted one of the freed American hostages as saying that during his captivity he had reevaluated his priorities and had engaged in a great deal of religious introspection while being held a prisoner in Iran. Perhaps Neven was also one of that gentleman's angels.

The guides often repeated themselves, stressing a point over and over again, much the same our teachers did when we were in school. Two times two is four. Two times two is four. An adjective describes a noun. An adjective describes a noun. Amo, amas, amat. We learned basically by repetition so as to etch the facts into our memory banks.

William, Neven, et al. used the same teaching method, especially when expressing their concern for mankind, but however they altered their words, the message was the same. *"Each person must look to his own soul, to his own spiritual enlightenment." "Turn away from error thoughts and see the God within."*

Neven seemed to be on a stage giving a sermon when he wrote the following message: *"Mankind must flush away the garbage with which he has fed himself, the garbage in which he believes as though it were countless riches of gold. If man considers material accoutrements above the wealth of his soul, he is unhappy, sick, tormented, miserable, and knows not why such a calamity has befallen him. Foresight in the human being is difficult to realize.*

"It is imperative that as many souls as possible there on earth know of us so we can then guide them directly to expedite their development. Love, Neven."

A week later Neven abandoned his stern lectures and gave me some uplifting news. *"We are pleased to announce the army is growing—the army of God is rallying to the Truth. The conscience of mankind is at least beginning to question although not to the extent where the exact solution or avenue of action is yet recognized. Any glimmer in the darkness is a ray of hope for all mankind. Love, Neven."*

What global event had prompted Neven's heartening attitude I did not know, but it was clear something good had occurred somewhere in the world that had moved him to comment with such elation.

At this point, I indulged in some interesting imagery. Just suppose within the next twenty-four hours every person on this planet tuned into God and His angels, the Spirit Guides, and followed their advice.

In my case, the woman next door would refrain from deliberately bringing her dogs on to my property. Because she will have acquired Divine Love, she would also have acquired consideration for others. My neighbor would turn down the volume on his stereo so never again would I be subjected to hearing only the wild beat of the drum throbbing like a never-ending tom-tom under my feet. Wailing sirens of ambulances and police cars would be silenced for there would be no crime, accidents, emergencies, or illnesses abroad in both material and spiritual realms.

We would all breathe clean air, drink pure refreshing water, and eat uncontaminated food. We would love our fellow man; love all things; we would know infinite joy.

Indulge a bit in your own imagery, pertaining to *your* daily life, then you have some idea of what the world would be like if each of us would listen, learn, and act according to God's word and His angels.

In February, Ondaras made a surprise appearance in my writing to emphasize the destiny of this planet: *"The world will become paradise when mankind learns to see God and His light. Each mortal must look within himself. Each one must tend to his own soul and clean out the debris which has too long rotted and become fetid. Why must man hang onto something which does him more ill than good? Why, indeed, because of vanity; because he feels he must satisfy his (mortal) desires which are placed with a mistaken emphasis of importance. Man creates his own destruction, his own punishment, yet he is all too willing to place the blame in every corner except where the fault truly belongs—on his own head, in his own mind, on his uncontrolled thoughts and desires.*

"The winds of ill blow strong in many corners of the world. Man must protect himself by joining the Divine Source of good, with God, the One Creator.

"To constantly seek growth in spiritual enlightenment is the quintessence of life on planet Earth. Believe, have faith and all good will come to the world. Love and Blessings, Ondaras."

Chapter 13

~

Marcus Aurelius, the Stoic emperor who reigned over Rome from A.D. 161 to A.D. 180, wrote in his Meditations: "Love mankind; follow God. The universe loves to make whatever is about to be. I say then to the universe that I love as thou lovest."

At the very onset of my automatic writing the word *love* appeared profusely. Always my angels ended their transcriptions with the word *love* preceding their signature. Over and over they stressed love. *"Learn to love; learn and love each day,"* they wrote. *"Love the world; love all things."* Constantly the angels urge me to *"Find love and truth; love is woven in the fabric of truth. Seek to know love and truth."*

I love my husband and my two sons with a deep, joyful devotion that emanates from the very core of my being. I feel the same about my granddaughter and daughters-in-law. I love my sister, my stepsons and their families, my nieces, my aunt, and my cousins. I love my close friends. Why, then, did the guides urge me to love? I confess to a slight case of defensive and "righteous" indignation toward their belaboring on love.

I *do* love, I protested to the guides. I love the roar of the ocean as it crashes against the craggy rocks of Leo Carillo Beach. I love the stark San Gabriel Mountains which form a permanent mural beyond my bedroom windows. I love the wheeling graceful arc of a seagull in flight. I love the scraggly squatty chapparal; the sentinel-like Joshua trees of the Mojave Desert. I love babies, aircraft, chocolate, writing, people, adventure. How could the angels, for one moment, think I do not love? "I love!" I told them. "I love, can't you see that? Surely *you* know I love!"

Neven, Van, Mother, and Ondaras overlooked my exhortations. Each day in my writing came additional references to learning love. *"You must learn love,"* they wrote, *"to love the world, love all things, love the enemy."*

The enemy? I have no enemies of which I am aware. I fight no battles. I am quite sure there are people who may not like me when we meet; I am too realistic to reject that possibility. But I would not classify those people as enemies.

"Love the world. Love all things. Love the enemy," the guides repeated.

For days I pondered my angels' ongoing messages

on loving the enemy. Then, I faced a severe test. Life, the university of the soul, is rife with tests. God and the angels spring surprise "quizzes" from time to time and this one I nearly flunked.

During the more than five years we lived in this apartment, the woman who owned the apartment building across the alley herded her two toy poodles behind *our* building for them to do their business. Intermittently, as I took out our trash, I caught her urging the dogs onto *this* property. Although a city ordinance requires dog owners to clean up after their pets, she never complied.

One day I pointed out her neglect. In a high shrill voice, she let loose a tirade of foul language. I stood nose-to-nose with her, not swearing, but shouting on an equal decibel level, telling her she had no consideration for others and that she was breaking the law. How would she like it if we all brought our dogs to defecate on *her* property? I was furious!

The shouting match did nothing but escalate my blood pressure and make me feel dreadful afterward. As far as I could see, it had no effect whatsoever on the woman. She continued bringing her nasty little dogs onto the asphalt drive behind our building.

"Love all things because all things are of God," my angels advised me at the next day's writing session. *"God is love and love is God. Love the enemy."*

Shortly after this message appeared, I had occasion

to once again take out the trash when my neighbor was there with her dogs.

Stifling a roar of frustration and anger, I remembered the admonishment of the angels: *"Love the enemy."*

Silently I said to myself as I approached the woman, All right, here is the enemy. I am supposed to love this thoughtless woman and her two undisciplined dogs. But, oh, God, how do I go about it?

The only way I knew how to cope without losing my temper was to pray. While holding the trash bag, I silently pleaded for the strength to love as the angels told me I should. This woman is a child of God just as I. I asked for the will to summon the spiritual power within me, the power of Divine Love.

"Hello." I spoke to the woman, who eyed me warily as though posing for battle while the yapping dogs circled my ankles readying an attack. The woman did not answer. I smiled and concentrated on visualizing my body generating love vibrations. I didn't know whether it would work or not, but I learned more about vibrations from my angels at each writing.

Soon, very soon, I felt the warmth of the energy and saw the vibrations with my inner eye as they radiated from my body. Love floated across the few yards separating us and wrapped itself around her like a gossamer cape. For extra measure, I sent a ray or two toward the dogs.

While radiating all that love, I kept in mind these words I received from William several days earlier: *"The key to a good and happy spirit and soul for all time is love. Love in the heart; love in the soul to put away forever the petty things of the world."*

Keeping my smile in place, I summoned stronger vibrations. The woman said nothing. The scowl did not disappear from her face, but she dug two tissues from her pocket, picked up the feces, and deposited it in *our* bin instead of her own. (At least she picked up.) I smiled brightly and disposed of my trash. Hurrying away, she called the dogs to follow her.

I returned to my apartment more than a little exhausted. Facing the test seemed difficult that first time, very difficult, believe me. A great surge of energy prevented me from criticizing the woman, and an equal if not greater amount expended to focus my thoughts in order to see this woman as a perfect soul, a child of God, as we all are; a soul who does not recognize her spiritual heritage, who is so caught up in the temporal world she is blinded to what she really is, a spiritual being who is part of God and in whom God dwells.

What part of me needed that same lesson? Evidently my angels knew and, not so subtly, reminded me from time to time. Understanding came ever so slowly to me, but the angels would not let me rest.

Several weeks later Van made a surprise appearance in my writing, sending an extended message full of sound advice: *"Feel the vibrations of love and use them each day with all you meet. The person may not be wise to the nature of the rays but they will feel a warmth in them.*

"Use every moment the truths you have learned; go out and show by your actions that God is love and you are God and you love all things. You must shine the light of love on as many as possible so they will begin to feel the glory of love that is God.

"Some minds will remain shut," Van concluded, *"but they will not escape the love vibrations. Many hours and days may pass before they understand. Get ye out to mankind and tell them of Divine Love, Divine Truth, and Divine Law."*

During the next writing session Neven continued on the subject of love: *"The message we have for all mankind is to love, learn, and grow. Ah, but the mortal forgets what True Divine Love means, and many times can only guess at what that love means. To love all things; not just those persons or objects of one's own personal preference, but to love everything, for each is made of God—all is made of God.*

"The message is clear and not difficult to understand. If just one thing you detest then you detest God. Is this not so since all is of God?

"Love is the key and most patience is required to halt the confusions caused by worldly thinking clashing with the spiritual thinking. Love is the key; love all things and you will know God."

If we would, all of us, but heed the words of the angels and the Bible concerning Divine Love! Love. Love. Love would conquer all the world's ills. True Divine Love would keep a would-be robber or murderer from attacking; love would prevent kidnapping, greed, malice. All-encompassing Divine Love would avert war and violence. All mankind would live in a heaven on earth—an earth ruled by Divine Love.

"Tell the world about us," my guides stressed, *"so mankind will seek God and turn to us to learn to love all things. We are ever vigilant to hear the call, to help you learn love in God's name."*

Several months later, to no doubt emphasize the importance of love to the human race and to all creatures, Neven reprised his message on love.

"Love is the most important attribute in all the universe—next to God, of course, but then God is love so it is of the same.

"You are confronted very often with human beings who give forth vibrations of evil, hatred, and venom. You know you are affected by them—by the person and their vibrations—unless you counteract and render them impotent of negativity by overpowering them with love. To those, one must offer special tolerance. Love is the key. Yes, love is the key to open the hearts of all mankind. You would do well to make that the focus of an entire chapter of your book. Love is the true essence of Spirit."

Neven seemed to have more to say. My arm ached

from the writing, but Neven wanted to finish his lecture so I again put pen to paper. *"If one cannot love— especially those who give him a difficult test, then one does not yet live in Spirit. By love we conquer the evil created in the mortal consciousness that has the appearance of frequenting the earth. Love even those who may try to harm you.*

"It is not demanded that you like the person but that you send energies of love to surround him. Divine Love, which is, oh, so different from personal love, the fleeting love humans bandy about so superficially in the name of Love. 'Fair weather love,' like 'fair weather friends,' has no credulity at all. It fails. Never could it be labeled love in the first place, but a carnal emotion, an emotion of material man, sensate man.

"Divine Love for all things is a fulfilling vibration, overwhelming in its power and is attainable by all mankind if he but destroy his personal ego and turn to Spirit."

A few days after the reception of that particular message, I experienced a strange urge to attend a nearby metaphysical church, not really knowing anything about their concept. I had seen the building many times in passing, but this time it seemed to call me in. Later, I realized that urge as the angels literally pushing me in the door of the sanctuary, for I discovered the minister spoke somewhat like my angels, AND, the title of his topic? LOVE! I wrote down his exact words on the margin of the bulletin.

"Divine Love," he said, "is not to be doled out

sparingly and irrationally here and there, flung at one and then another, flung at some and not others. Love should emanate so strongly, the persons receiving it step forward to be absorbed into its radiant light."

It is often difficult to express Divine Love unless you keep constant harmony and balance with God and the universe. One's patience is sorely tried when a thousand dollars' worth of music equipment is stolen from your husband's car. It tests one's soul when graffiti is spray-painted on a garage wall; when violence becomes the norm in the media and the movies. It is irksome when one is confronted with a querulous neighbor each day, but Neven repeatedly told me to love all things and see each creature in the light of the Divine. He warned me not to let another person gain control of my emotions by giving them up. Faith and love, he advised, can conquer the tests which mortal man must face to learn and grow.

Neven became unusually poetic at his next writing. *"Love is the blanket that warms the soul; love is the manna which keeps the soul fed. Love is the music of the universe; the ultimate joy for God is all love. Dance, then, for the joy of Divine Love and fret not to gain only mortal love which is destructible and soon turns to ashes. The stalwart sturdy Divine Love is all-pervading and knows nothing of a jealous heart or a selfish possession or unbridled passion or foolish vanity. Love is God and you are love just as you are God.*

"Everything in the universe is God, is made by God, for God," Neven continued. *"If God is love, which He truly is, then God is made by love, God is love, God is for love. There is no difference. They flow together as the drops in a stream which mingle and flow.*

"When all mankind turns to Divine Love—then will the battle be won and all will return to God's intention of love. Love all things and you learn the truth and the truth frees you from bondage. Your soul will soar and you will know God. Love, love, love, Neven."

How does one acquire love? According to my angels, it must develop in the heart and soul by daily allowing God to pour out his Divine Love on us; by sincere prayer and a belief that we are one with the perfect love of God, the One Creator, and asking that we express His Divine Love at all times.

Thus in my daily prayers I ask that the love of God envelop me, that I give expression to God's love at all times. Many times I meditate on the God of Love which is in each human being on earth.

Love cannot be measured with a caliper or amplified by laser. Love cannot be photographed either by a camera or x-rays. Mortal love or Divine Love, neither can be defined with scientific instruments nor charted on a graph. Love is a divine attribute developed through prayer, meditation, and affirmation.

One of my favorite meditations, by Yogananda, the famed Indian master who founded the Self-Realization Fellowship, reads, "Let love spread its laughter in all our hearts, in every person belonging to every race. Let love rest in the hearts of flowers, of animals and of little specks of stardust."

The meditation on love I will cherish forever is the one originating with my own angel guide, Neven: *"Love is the blanket that warms the soul."*

Chapter 14

If love is the blanket that warms the soul, then truth is the lamp that lights the path to the mountain of spiritual knowledge. Many months of writing and studying passed before the true light of Truth illumined my path, which not only wound around like a maze, but also became rife with the tangled undergrowth of misconception.

Each one of my guardian angels, whether William, Mother, Van, or Ondaras, from the beginning urged me to seek the divine attributes of Love and Truth. Neven, on his appearance in my writing, took up the banner. Eventually, through their wisdom and guidance, I learned the meaning of Divine Love. Discovering Divine Truth and being able to comprehend the true from the false became another matter entirely, a very serious and difficult matter. Before my discovery of Divine Truth, written with a capital *T*, I knew only truth written with a small *t*.

Divine Truth indicates spiritual perfection, wholeness. Divine Truth never changes for it is a spiritual law, a law of the universe. Your spiritual self never changes. Within you, within your soul, if you will, all is well, infinitely. You are perfect, whole, complete.

The word, *truth*, with the lowercase *t*, means a fact, the state of things as they appear at the moment. But facts can and do change. It may be a fact that you have a cold. It may be a fact you have no job. Your age is a fact. Statistics are facts. The truth is you may be in debt, but that fact could change with changing circumstances.

For further in-depth explanation one must seek out and read many metaphysical books that are available. Early in my automatic writing, I believed only facts were the truth. It took many sessions of the writing, a lot of reading, consistent prayer, and meditation to find the Truth, all of which were orchestrated by my angels.

In writing of Divine Love and Divine Truth, the guides refrained from indulging in any suggestion of frivolity. Succinct commands came through in the early stages of the writing, mainly from William who sounded very much like a father laying down rules and regulations to his child. *"Look for Truth." "Learn to tell only the Truth." "Let Truth come into your soul."*

"Seek the real Truth and learn to tell real Truth from false." "Learn the Truth and tell the world."

The orders were definite—learn Truth. How to go about the task caused me great bewilderment. How would I know whether something was the real Truth or disguised as Truth? Would I be able to distinguish real Truth from non-Truth? What if I interpreted something as Truth and it was not?

When faced with a dilemma, I consult the angels. *"How do I go about learning the real Truth?"* I asked William. He replied, *"Pray to God for guidance and seek in many places. Each day pray and you will find what you seek. Learn to read the Truth."*

The order seemed easy to accomplish, at least the part about praying. I pressed William further. "How might I learn to read Truth?" I inquired.

William responded eloquently, *"You will know by the light sent to your mind and soul."*

As I discovered much later, he was absolutely right.

Following William's orders I prayed daily for guidance and for Divine Wisdom in sorting out all the data presented in my studies in order for me to be able to discern spiritual Truth.

God's answer did not come immediately. Scheduled for many months of further in-depth study, meditation, and prayer, I thus faced a test of perseverance. Then slowly, very slowly, the answers appeared and by the light sent to my mind and soul, I knew, I understood Truth.

The first real Truth I discovered had to do with Christ. If I were to stop ten people on the street and ask each of them, "What do you associate with the word *Christ*; what does the word *Christ* mean?" the odds are great that all ten would immediately answer "*Jesus.*" I probably would have given that answer before my angels taught me the word *Christ*, which embraces far more than a singular identity or entity.

Christ was not Jesus' last name. His father and mother were not Mr. and Mrs. Joseph Christ. Jesus' middle name was not Christ. The Greek word *christos* existed in language long before Jesus' birth, as did the Latin word *christus*.

Definitively, the word *Christ* is a title meaning *anointed*. It signifies an ideal prototype of humanity; the one complete idea of perfect man. Your higher self, my higher self, the higher self or Spiritual Self of all life is the Christ-consciousness within each of us. Jesus expressed the pure personification of the I Am or the Jehovah within each human being. Jesus exemplifies the complete embodiment of the divine attributes man must emulate if he is to unify himself with God. Jesus, the individual expression of Christ-consciousness, did not have the title, Christ, bestowed on him until several years after his death. According to Biblical scholars, the disciple, Peter, called him Christ because of Jesus' spiritual perception.

My guardian angels led me to the right books, the right teachers from whom I learned more and more of Truth.

With the following message signed by Mother, my angels applauded my concerted effort to learn Truth. *"You give much joy to God and to us in all your learning. Be of good heart, be patient, and you learn many more things."* Patiently, as instructed, and now with consuming interest, I continued my education under the expert tutelage of my Spirit Guides, angels in the army of God.

Man, in his true essence and in reality, I learned, is a spiritual being. His true origin is in Spirit, thus his inherent nature is spiritual. Man's physical nature is transitory; his spiritual nature is eternal.

Where did mankind go wrong? If man were sent to earth to express his spiritual nature as his primary concern, why do we now place the spiritual secondary in our lives? Because in its mortal state, with its temptations and distractions, mankind developed a consciousness apart from the spiritual. The world today finds itself in dire circumstances because of that flagrant mistake. As the population of this planet multiplied, so did erroneous thoughts and erroneous beliefs until an imbalance between the spiritual and the mortal caused disharmony with the Cosmic or Divine Law. Such disharmony bred illness, disease, crime, war, hate, distrust, mistakes, and a further growth of erroneous thoughts in the human race.

The question becomes—are we to totally refute our societal existence, cloister ourselves in a cave, become incommunicado with the rest of mankind and do nothing but meditate, pray, and focus our entire attention on our own personal spiritual growth without any thought of sharing or using our knowledge to be of service to others?

According to my guardian angels, whom I approached with this question, to shut one's self away from the world creates the same confusion and degree of disharmony as totally ignoring the spiritual and only feeding physical desires while embracing the material world as the only reality.

Neven jumped right in with eloquence. *"Total absorption with the spiritual without thought given to everyday concerns is disruptive to equal balance. You see, dear child, if each who contacts us shuts himself off from the physical world and creates a world around us and himself only, he either misinterprets our messages or he does not understand the point we make.*

"We here would be in a sad state indeed if each mortal wrapped himself around with a noose of absorption, submerging himself so deeply he gives himself no chance for further growth by putting what he has learned into practice.

"A monk cloistered in his cell alone for many years

may realize much about himself but his spiritual growth decelerates if he does not use the knowledge to help others.

"A mortal lives on earth to not only seek and learn but also to put into practice the very things he has learned. The last is what speeds his growth. All souls, carnate and discarnate, must band together—the army of God—to spread the word throughout the world.

"On the other side of the scale is sensate man who bolts shut the door of his narrow mind and dwells in a cramped cell of debauchery, pettiness, and atheism. He selfishly feeds his five senses, satisfying only material desires. Each minor incident in everyday life takes on an aura of grand importance to the detriment of his spiritual life. Material possessions become his God; the external beauty of his physical body, his temple. He savagely grinds his inherent spiritual nature under the heel of his grimy boot of ignorance.

"The illusory permanence of his day-to-day world is false, fleeting. In Divine Truth only his soul is eternal. Until he crucifies, abandons his error thoughts and beliefs, he cannot begin to understand what he is fully capable through his spiritual nature of coming into Divine Harmony, Divine Unity with God.

My angels often have a word or two to say about balance and harmony. William, at one time early in my writing wrote this:

"Bring yourself into harmony to clear the channels of communication. Keep the channels open and listen carefully. Continually keep in balance to stay in tune with

God. To acquire good mental health, physical health, and spiritual health, one must discipline himself to stay in balance."

To balance a seesaw, weight must be evenly distributed on both sides of the fulcrum. If the old-fashioned scales, the type held by the statue of Justice, are not balanced equally on each of the plates, erroneous measurement results. In relating this premise to our modern world, we could substitute the word *moderation* for balance to further amplify the definition.

In politics, the fanatical dogma of the far right is every bit as dangerous as the zealous tenet of the far left. Bringing the premise "closer to home," a person who nearly starves himself to the point of emaciation damages his health to the same degree as one who gorges himself on food and drink. To cause imbalance in *any* facet of life, whether temporal, ethereal, cerebral, emotional, physical, or mental is perilous. Keeping one's self balanced and harmonious with God and Its nature leads to acceleration of spiritual growth.

Ondaras, in an all too infrequent appearance in the writing, began a transcription with these words: *"The universe vibrates and those who place themselves in tune with like vibrations clear the air for proper communication with God, the God within. The God in all things, the God in each person, in all things of the universe throbs with the pulsating vibrations. Nothing is motionless. Tune yourself with this vibration more finely. Cast away those adverse vibrations that do not balance and meld so you can swim with the current."*

Never doubting my guardian angels, I always travel with the direction they suggest. If a particular book comes my way, I read it carefully, subsequently discovering the message I know my guides were confident I would find. Early in my automatic writing, while complying with their orders to read the Bible, I came across Proverbs 4:23: "Be careful how you think; your life is shaped by your thoughts."

With that verse, I learned the Truth of Spiritual Law which is the Law of Cause and Effect. What you think is what you will get, no matter how sublimated the thought. If you worry constantly about the possibility of becoming ill, more than likely you will become ill. If you believe something bad is going to happen in your life, it will manifest according to the degree of your belief. If you believe you will always be poor, you probably will always be poor. What you feed into God's heavenly computer, your subconscious, is exactly what will return according to the depth of your conviction. If you think negative thoughts, you get negative results; if you think positive thoughts, you get positive results. The Spiritual Law of Cause and Effect.

The angels taught me very well. They sent many messages relaying this idea. Rather than curse God for your misfortune, learn to control your thoughts for that is where it originates. Proverbs 13:3 reads:

"Be careful what you say and protect your life. A careless talker destroys himself."

Whether thinking or voicing thoughts, the Law of Cause and Effect applies. God's Spiritual Law is the only True Law. I learned another fact of Truth my guardian angels commanded me to seek.

Chapter 15

Nightmares seldom invade my dreams. Weird dreams, yes. Distorted dreams, yes. But not terrifying dreams, the kind that, even though you wake up, makes your body tremble, wraps you like a shroud in a deep sense of foreboding.

I awakened with a start shortly after midnight early one Sunday in January 1981. A great sense of fear gripped me. I had dreamed something terrible concerning my 33-year-old son, Rick. In vain I tried recalling specifics of the dream. Two hours later, after I once again fell asleep, the same dream jarred me awake. I remembered nothing. Twice more that night I bolted upright, frightened from the same sense of horror.

At 4:30 A.M. I made the wise decision to consult my guardian angels. Sitting at the dining room table in a warm robe and slippers, I wrote: "I am open to your guidance with loving thanks."

Neven lost no time in conveying this message: *"It is imperative that you impress on son with all possible speed and emphasis, he does not enter into that which he now contemplates. Tell him it is much too complicated, devious and, yes, dangerous. If he is to accomplish his goal in life, he must resist all temptation to which he could easily succumb."*

My heart pounded loudly. Rick! In danger! Always adventuresome, always the daredevil, on many occasions he defied conventional rules. Immediately, I sent Neven this question, "What is Rick thinking of entering?"

Neven answered quickly. *"Your lot is to warn him and not enter into specifics. He will know of that which I speak.*

"He must not—and we cannot stress strongly enough—he MUST NOT enter into that plan which would destroy his ambition, destroy his freedom, destroy his self-esteem. If he is to conquer all his problems and all his fears and worries, he MUST listen to us or all is lost for this life."

My hand trembled. I could hardly go on but I knew I must. *"Son has tremendous potential that he is eroding by self-abuse, unwise decisions, and irresponsible actions. Man is tempted heavily many times but one must resist no matter how alluring or attractive the trip.*

"On his present path, if he succumbs to continual temptation, there is nothing but total destruction ahead. What

a waste that would be for one so loved, so talented and, yes, so spiritually advanced if he would but see."

My face burned with fear. My hands shook. Rick faced danger of some dire kind for Neven had never been that strongly adamant as in this warning.

"Waste not a minute"—Neven dictated urgently as I started writing once again—*"to get the message to him. Do not chide, do not beg. You are but a messenger. If he does not heed our word, you do nothing but cry in your heart. He must decide. Love, Neven."*

Dropping the pen, I lowered my head, said an earnest prayer for Rick, and cried. I cried from fear, exhaustion, lack of sleep, and more fear.

What could I do? Rick, I knew, spent every weekend with his bride-to-be. Never ever had I called him there. I wouldn't now, not at seven o'clock on a Sunday morning. Whatever the problem it could wait another hour or so, maybe even until noon.

"No!" The voices of my guides, all of them, resounded in my inner ear. *"NOW!"* they chorused.

When Rick answered the phone I apologized and explained the circumstances. Well aware of my angels and the writing, he listened quietly as I read Neven's message word-for-word. After I finished, he remained silent for a long moment, then, very quietly, said, "Thanks, Mom, and thank your kids for me. I'll call you later. I love you."

Sunday, for me, became agonizing. I chewed my nails, paced the floor, and held long conversations with myself. Maybe I had misinterpreted the message. Maybe Rick planned something insignificant but risky. He seemed to live on the edge and take undue chances. Perhaps I should have waited to call. Maybe whatever the problem, it would take place Monday or Tuesday or even Wednesday.

No, the angel, Neven, had said *now* and that I must make haste to get the message to Rick. Oh, God, please let him listen to the message and take heed, as Neven had urged. The day dragged slowly along.

The telephone rang at exactly seven P.M. Rick said, "We're back!"

"Back from where?" I asked with great joy.

"From Ojai. We took the dog, drove the truck, and spent the day in the mountains."

"Rick, maybe the message from Neven didn't mean today. Maybe it was—"

He interrupted. "No, Mom, it was today. And I didn't do it."

I heard myself sigh with relief. "Well, I'm happy about that. I don't need to know any more."

"No, I want you to know. You deserve to know," he said. "At one o'clock this afternoon I was to drive a van load of drugs to New York and get a bundle of cash when I got there.

"I might not have heeded Neven's warning if Debbie hadn't awakened me just five minutes before you called. She said a terrible nightmare had awakened her. It was something frightening about me, something dangerous, but she couldn't remember any of the dream. She just felt frightened. She had the same bad dream as you, Mom.

"I might make mistakes at times and seem pretty stupid but I couldn't ignore the strong evidence that your angels were watching over me and warning me.

"I'm in no danger. I'm okay and I've learned a big lesson."

My Guardian Angels never predict. They say to tell someone's future is taking away a person's choice, but the angels do warn, strongly, about an impending problem or danger. Thank you, Neven, Mother, Van, and Ondaras for saving my son. I will never forget you are always with me and mine.

Chapter 16

Four months and six days after his first transcription, Neven, without a word of warning, disappeared from my group of angels. When Ondaras signed the next two messages in succession, I should have expected the change. Not until Ondaras's third message did I know Neven had moved on.

"The lessons you learn every day are the collective works of all of us. Just one does not give advice exclusively, the work is a group effort even though each has a specific assignment to fulfill at certain times. Although Neven is gone, like William, he, too, has himself tuned so he knows of your progress. Some will not stay forever with you for they also have other assignments when they have fulfilled their duties on your behalf.

"You by now know you are not to be alarmed by this natural progression for it is the divine order of things. As you progress, others step in to guide you further. Each of

us has its particular assignment as far as it concerns your spiritual growth.

"As you look back over the past months and the messages, you get a broader view of your progress and also of us here. We, also, have gone forward and it is with unbounded joy that we so report.

"As you would say, others are 'waiting in the wings' to come to your aid at the appropriate moment. You will know full well when that happens. You will know that it is another step forward for you and for us as well.

"If you are perplexed or have a question or doubt in your mind of anything, do not hesitate to ask. Bring it forward for when it is brought to the open before you, it facilitates our answering and your understanding.

"You will get much important help in the next few days," Ondaras assured me. "Listen, feel, concentrate, meditate, and gather the thoughts which are prone to wander like wild mustangs in the open prairie. Your thoughts must be corralled and sifted to make better use of them.

"Do not fret about the book. You will accomplish all you wish for. Keep love in your heart. Keep your sights on the mountaintop and bask forever in God's light. Love, Ondaras."

The next day, as I sat at my desk awaiting the angels' dictation, I fully expected to hear from my new guide, whomever would appear. Ondaras had further information for me.

"Neven says you will do well to go on with your studies," Ondaras wrote. "He has been called on an urgent *matter elsewhere. You will have a new guide and, as usual, I shall be in charge of your progress.*

"Remember to have patience in all things; remain calm in upheaval and love all things, even those who try your soul.

"The name of your new guide is Merlin. He will do much to give you much information for your books and is quite good at many things. The messages will go fast. Your fortune improves greatly and you are on your way. Have you noticed a more positive stature in your actions and thoughts? Merlin, in orienting himself as your current instructor, has playfully tried an experiment or two with your lessons."

Merlin! So I had a jester on my hands. As for his experiments, I did recall that for several days before, the world seemed unusually rosy and bright. I found many things to make me laugh and many things pleased me. Even household chores seemed less tiresome. My approach to housework has never been merry. Welcome into my life, Merlin.

Ondaras continued his transcription. *"By now you know how natural it is to experience new teachers so we need not give you a long dissertation of assurance that this is natural and will continue. You benefit greatly from the different kinds of help you will receive. Mother and Van say they are also here as 'stabilizers' so that constant new voices will give you no concern. You will not feel lost knowing they are yet among your group of angels. To them their most important work is with you—they need not go elsewhere. However, William and Neven must needs travel to other projects of utmost importance where they are more sorely needed. Love, Ondaras."*

Merlin indeed presented a drastic change from any other of my angels. From this complete first message from Merlin you may judge for yourself. *"Now we will get to know each other and come up with some fine ideas for your writing. Please do not be upset that I am come to replace Neven for a time. Each of us has his particular forte to help you along in specific areas.*

"Things are going well, are they not? You can feel the glory of life and it is something you wish all the world to share. And you will, you will, for you will write in a manner that everyone can enjoy and understand.

"We here are nothing to be frightened of nor are we the least bit mysterious. Those poor souls who deem you daft for believing in us and who label us a figment of your imagination are to be pitied for their narrow minds. Any joy they might think they have in life is artificial joy, forced upon themselves because they think they should be happy and wish they could be happy.

"Figments of your imagination! Indeed we are not! Our dimension is far from being imagination. We live to the fullest degree. If only poor earth souls would broaden their minds and hearts, then they would meet us and know the true meaning of joy in God. We are not figments. Rigid mind are FIGS when they are MEANT to be noble spiritual children of God. You did not miss my little play on words there, now, did you?

"You see we are happy here and we take great joy in making earth people happy. Some of us seem not to be serious but we are, and we can whisper all the philosophies at you, just like the others, but we do not work that way. By we I mean those of us who on earth might be called jesters.

"Life need not be solemn simply because it is serious. We shout, turn flips, laugh and play in the glory that is God. One should not find pain on the path nor be glum. God's love tickles us with such overwhelming joy, we delight in it all.

"I think my point for today is—solemnity doesn't mean a person is religious. Being good does not necessarily mean you are spiritual. Being cantankerous doesn't mean you are all bad. The Truth is we are all love and love is God. When a soul sees that, his only aim is to act like God. Be joyful, praise Him, and keep the lamp high.

"I will be here each day for a while and we will explore much joy together. You laugh good and I shall laugh with you. Bushels of blessings. Love, Merlin."

Although I could scarcely believe what I read, the personality of Merlin came through as quite refreshing. Was he the soul of Merlin, the court magician, of the legend of King Arthur? Perhaps the story was not legend at all. Could a court magician also be a court jester? It seemed to me Merlin must have been a comedian in a recent lifetime. My new angel got the ball bouncing right off the bat at the next day's writing session. *"Now we sit down to start the lesson for today and it is titled DOUBT versus FAITH or BELIEF versus DISBELIEF. You harbor doubts occasionally, doubts that you may not be going in the right direction, doubts that you may not be capable of the task we ask of you.*

"YOU know you have doubts at one time or another and WE know it. Get rid of those doubts this very second and have faith. How can you doubt and have faith at the same time? It is impossible—just as you cannot believe in something and not believe in it at the same time. There is not room for both in your soul. It is simple—get rid of doubt. If it sneaks up on you, smash it down and throw it out. You need not burden yourself with such a load of garbage.

"You say you believe—believe in God, believe in us, yet you allow doubts to creep into your mind. If you believe, truly believe, it is impossible to doubt, so do away with doubt and disbelief forever. So much for that lesson. Learn it and you are on your way in a flash of light."

Here I paused to rest, for Merlin, in his transcription, sent messages very fast but never with a mocking or adamant tone. His vibrations flowed effortlessly with warmth, love, and joy, with always a hint of excitement to come. He seemed in such a hurry to tell me all he wished me to know.

"You wonder who I am and where I came from and did we ever know each other. Oh, I have been around in your lives—hardly ever a close friend but hovering on the fringes of a crowd around you. I made you smile, I made

you laugh, and I rejoiced to see you happy. And in more than one time past I have comforted you when you were sad, held your hand when you were frightened, and pointed the way when you were lost."

Everyone should have a friend like Merlin, a friend near at hand to help wherever and whenever he could. He said we were not close friends. I wonder what kind of person I might have been in our lifetime together if I could not take such a warm and caring soul as a dear and trusted friend. His following story on one of our past lives together nearly made me cry.

"As childhood chums in one life we got lost together in a dark woods but I sang for you and told funny stories so you would not be afraid. I told you never to doubt we would be found and we were. The chief sent out many braves from the camp to find us. A sweet little girl you were, but when you became a big woman you were taken by another man for his wife."

Each time I read Merlin's story, tears well up. The long-suffering suitor thwarted in his love for a young girl apparently insensitive to the deep emotions of the young man who joked and laughed; a soul who ever played the clown.

My angel, Merlin, continued his message: *"Always on the fringes of your lives watching over you. I rejoice when you rejoice and doubly happy am I to take this assignment. Do not be frightened when I become a more strict teacher as I will at times for that is my nature, just as it is also my nature to be jovial. I want you to learn very much and to complete this important project of the book then send it out when the world hungers to know of us.*

"Do not wince if you are sometimes ridiculed for your belief in us. Many have carried that burden down the ages of time. It is of no consequence, for you know the Truth and the maligners are the losers.

"Tomorrow, more for the book. We all send much love, Merlin."

With the advent of Merlin, the writing took on a sense of urgency and a definite hurried "bounciness" I am sure the reader is able to detect. While the other angels took much time to send what they wanted to convey, Merlin seemed in such a rush to tell me so much.

Sometimes I wrote at night, after readying myself for bed. The night following the preceding message, Merlin seemed to be chattering all the while I brushed my teeth. I could make out "get going" and "hurry, hurry, much to say." Finally, I said aloud, "Hold on, Merlin, will you please? I'll be with you in a minute."

From the living room my husband shouted, "Were you talking to me?"

"No, honey, it's Merlin. He's impatient for me to learn more."

"Well, you'd better get at it then and not keep Merlin waiting," Ron answered.

The instant I put pen to paper, the writing started.

"At this time, dear one," Merlin began, "we will discuss nourishment—food; food for the body and food for the soul.

"For the body to sustain life, it must be fed and watered. If one does not tend to feeding the body, it dies and turns all its chemical and mineral components back to the earth.

"Why is it that some human beings are constantly discomfitted with illness? He does not abstain from ingesting poisons. A healthy body opens the channels to us. Your mind, on all its levels, becomes more aware. Clean up dietary habits, environmental toxins, and purify.

"The second reason for illness is putrid error thoughts which contaminate the mind just as toxic foods contaminate the body. One must go on a mental diet if he is to eliminate illness in his mind, which is a major cause of illness in the body. Neither is easy if a person thinks of only satisfying his passionate desires as though he were king. Feeding natural food to the soul is more important than feeding the body naturally. But, yea, they should go hand-in-hand. All people on earth should be exceedingly alert to what their minds ingest, what their bodies ingest, and what their souls ingest.

With Merlin shouting in my ear most of the day I had a constant reminder to purify my system further. I had to quit smoking. I knew it would be a bad habit of the past. About my soul, well, it might not hurt to look into nurturing it, too.

My peppy little angel concluded his message with: "You may think I travel too fast in these messages, which are extended. Time is of the essence because I shall be with *you just a short time for now. I am come to help you further your book project to tell the world about us. I shall return at a later time, so do not despair. Now that you are becoming used to the changes, you will notice more frequent replacing of your guides.*

"I might say here it is a heavenly pleasure that I am allowed to take part in and witness your growth. We have, for such a long time, as you there measure time, waited to enroll you in our classes and embrace you into an awareness of God's universe. We are well pleased and all send their joy and blessings. Love, Merlin."

Was this Merlin's farewell speech? It seemed so. Accustomed to replacement angels by this time, I wished Merlin well on his new assignment. He promised he would one day return so I let him go with ease, looking forward to the next angel in the army of God.

At my next writing session, expectantly awaiting a new guide, I recognized Merlin's transcription vibrations immediately. He came right to the point. *"This book project is nearing completion. It is well that this one ends with me as your guide, is it not? For we have much to tell all people and you have been chosen to write this for us. You will do well to go over the entire volume and see how it has progressed. When you send it off to a place near you, then you can clear your mind and your desk and begin action on the next."*

Wait a minute here, Merlin. The next? I haven't a clue as to what I'm to do with this one. And how will this manuscript end if you leave now? What would a new book be about? How will I know . . . ? Oh, of course, you prolific angels would guide me through it, but I would like to have more specifics, please.

"You are thinking we do not let you rest but you have done groundwork on the second and will have much more resources coming your way. The second will be much easier than the first for each day you become more finely tuned."

Flattery got Merlin everywhere. Okay, so I would finish this and get on with the next. With the angels in the army of God leading the way and pushing me from behind at the same time, what else could I do? Their messages should reach all mankind for they wish to help, not only to aid mortals on their path, but to also spur forward their own spiritual growth. Merlin's final message eloquently summed up, for all mankind, a lesson in living.

"We have such wonderful goals for mankind and each person could be a part of it, as you well know. Does it sometimes seem impossible to convey the glory and joy to others? Ah, I know. They do not listen, for their rigid confined ideas have impaired their hearing, their grandiose attitudes have blinded their vision, and their obstinacy has hardened their hearts. They fear an idea they think not their own. Their mortal minds refute a premise they cannot understand or which frightens them.

"As God's disciples, we should frighten no one. There is never cause for fear. Fear is unknown in this realm and

should be unknown for mortals, but again, they shut their minds in a tiny room and bolt the door. All they can see is contained in that minute space. They must open wide the door, knock down the walls, and race with joy among the vibrations of God's universe.

"Talk to the trees and rocks, sing with praise to the sky and clouds, whisper love to the raindrops, embrace the rainbow arcing across God's heavens. By the same token, love the poor and needy, pray for the sick and wounded, stretch out a helping hand to the desolate. Meditate on all that is God."

My poet, Merlin. My humanitarian, Merlin. My teacher, Merlin. Comfort in his leaving came from his assurance that he would return. However, he had not yet finished this assignment, for the words flowed forth from my pen.

"My dear child, my soul is full of God's love and so should yours be. It is not an easy task in your dimension, but it is possible. Then you will know the complete joy and happiness I wish for you—we all wish for you and for all mankind.

"We are here and we are there all at the same time. We, not just your group, but all the guides of the universe eagerly await the recognition and the call for help. Man must enroll in our school to learn what he must know to cope with this time and eons ahead. We shall all work together to bring the earth once again to its place as the original Garden of Eden.

"Spiritual knowledge and education never ends and

isn't it marvelous? I laugh with you. I share your happiness. We will one day skip across God's heavenly pastures together sending our voices raining down on those who need our help. In the meantime, you have many years of earthly progress left and you will lead many to know of us.

"We are all proud of your accomplishment with this project. Ondaras says you get a top grade. Mother and Van smile with pride. It is done. You will tell the world of us. Blessings and joy. Love, Merlin."

Merlin was wrong. The project continued with a new angel.

Chapter 17

"*When the occasion seems right to you*," the message began, "*and something tells you to go ahead—gives you the green light, so to speak, then it is wise for you to do just that. You can help others to understand then you will do much to further your progress as well as theirs.*"

Ondaras? No, nor was it Van or Mother. Although William vowed to look in on me from time to time, the tone and style of the writing were not his, nor Neven's. The message seemed a bit prim for the vivacious Merlin, who had already bid me good-bye. A new voice was being heard. Who could it be?

In the eight days following Merlin's departure from my group of guardian angels, the writing produced four messages from Ondaras, three from Mother, and one from Van. Each message pertained to the acceleration of future transmissions, my spiritual growth, and the good fortune awaiting me in the days ahead if I chose to keep on my path of learning. The angels assured me they were constantly feeding me ideas to help with the project.

The new guide came in on the ninth day after Merlin took his leave. I told Ron, my husband, that this guide seemed to be some kind of professor with a rather stentorial tone, yet with vibrations of warmth. The no-nonsense approach and the speed of the transmission kept me ever alert yet I felt a deep sense of love and caring in the energy.

"You have done well learning to this point but never think for one moment you have come to the end of your learning for it is endless even though, eventually [will] come to the point where you dwell forever with God. Then there is no further need to attend earthly school for you become master teacher to all the students who are in dire need of education. That is the program here, the basic program, and all creatures would do well to learn that lesson.

"It is difficult to buck the tide, is it not? So many closed minds surround you at times, it is extremely difficult to keep your mind open and the channels clear. But one goal should always be uppermost in heart, soul, and mind—to be God-like, to love, always love even those who would do you ill, even those souls who are miserable and aim their misery at others. Misery and venom are caused, not by outer circumstance, but by inner error thoughts which are not discarded but allowed to ferment. That fermentation

is sent to every cell of the body and is a debilitating force to not only the physical body but it poisons the mind and infects the soul. Send love when you meet such a person, send love and subdue your vain ego. Keep control over your emotions and your thoughts and you emerge victorious."

The new guide, I reasoned, must have been a lecturer or teacher at one time. The tone, neither frivolous nor stern, lacked the panache of Merlin and the austerity of Ondaras, yet impressed me as being cordial. The angel transmitting had a sedate bearing yet was not unfriendly. Curiosity kept me writing longer than I intended, but the impetus to keep going emanated from the spirit guide itself.

"You by now know," the message went on, *"I have come as your new guide. I have had some time to observe while Neven and Merlin yet counseled you. I am well pleased with what I have seen and heard. The book shall not be totally finished yet, for I have a word or two to say and you may wish to incorporate my ideas in your current project.*

"You must give me free rein and refrain from incorporating your material ideas with mine. Your own mind thoughts may try to interfere from time to time but between us we shall erase them. You shall be able to recognize which are mine and what you think are your thoughts, but we shall control them.

"You are the medium through which we send these thoughts and you must not interfere with transmission by

forcing ideas which you, the medium, deem should be there. You do understand the reasoning behind this. I just wish to make sure all is understood and all is clear between us before we advance any further in your lessons. Now that the prelude is disposed of, shall we get down to the business at hand? You may sometimes rest if you so wish. The decision is yours and I shall wait until you are ready to once again take up the pen."

Whoever it might be, whatever its station, this angel's concern for my comfort was especially gratifying since my arm ached from the speed of the dictation. Who was this benevolent spirit so thoughtful of my welfare?

"You have many interests to pursue, therefore you may have given none a singular focus and concentration. That is why for years past you have been unable to hone and refine any. This is in no way a condemnation. Actually, all done before prepared you for this very stage in your development, although it may be difficult to discern."

Clearly this disparate guide knew me well, but then, if all spirit guides have access to all records, perhaps it was not a matter of familiarity but spiritual business acumen. Who was this astute, interesting angel giving the lecture? The next message brought the most welcomed answer.

"Do you remember when you were a child, not a tiny tot but in the junior high school? A very good student you were although many times you were distracted by your personality and your various interests. I am pleased

to know you learned a great deal in my English class. You did not know I kept a keen eye on you, for I could see the possibilities there. Yes, I taught you in seventh grade. Do you now remember? Of course you do, because through the years, whether you were conscious of it or not, you have realized the influence I had on you as your teacher.

"I am delighted to see you have not compromised the values you were taught although you must remember that for a few years of your life you were confused and got a bit off the track."

I could not deny the identity of this new guide—Miss Clark, my seventh-grade English teacher. She also served as head of my homeroom where we students of 7A kept our books, and gathered before class time to recite the Lord's Prayer and the Pledge of Allegiance to the flag. The students in other homerooms sat quietly during the five minutes between the flag ceremony and the sound of the first class bell. Not so in Miss Clark's homeroom. I recall the prim, colorless spinster relished giving mini-lectures on every subject imaginable, from proper etiquette to keeping oneself clean in body, heart, and mind.

Miss Clark wore no makeup. Her hair, gray-streaked, stacked high in a coiled bun atop her head. Shapeless somber-colored dresses hung unevenly below her knees. She became the butt of many a whispered joke behind her back. I joined in with my two cents' worth now and then, ridiculing her insistence on deportment, giggling at inordinately precise mannerisms.

But Miss Clark's students learned. Not until later years did we realize how much of Miss Clark's wisdom we had absorbed, despite our cruel and unwarranted criticism of her.

The writing continued: *"Brother remembers, too, and asks to be remembered to you. He recalls you as an impish joy. Spunk is the word he uses and we join in laughter at some of the memories we have shared. You did not know you afforded us such joy when we compared notes, did you?"*

Brother could be none other than Mr. Clark, my sixth-grade teacher, and Miss Clark's brother, who was also the principal of the elementary school I attended.

How strange he should label me impish and having spunk. I kept my precocious nature subdued as his student. Why? A large paddle hung from a nail by the door. Principal Clark doled out punishment for the entire school. Many times, after a whispered conversation with another teacher at our classroom door, Mr. Clark barked an order at us to study a certain chapter, took the ominous paddle from the hook, and closed the door behind him.

The wails of the offender and the sound of repeated whacks could be heard through the walls separating his office from our room. I vowed then and there to never misbehave as *his* student.

In her inimitable authoritative tone, Miss Clark once more took up the dictation. *"Well, now, shall we cease for this time and begin at a later date? You must be tired for this is quite a lecture which is typical of me. We are greatly pleased that you now take things in stride and are neither frightened nor mystified by our appearance in your life. Good! Then we shall get down to business at the next meeting. I have looked forward to once again having you as a student. Good night and we shall continue. All here send their love and blessings. They do love you very much, as I am sure you are aware. Until tomorrow. Love, Hannah."*

The unexpected signature leaped from the page. Hannah? Never did I ever call Miss Clark "Hannah." How interesting she chose to sign with her given name. Staring at the signature before me, I recalled the neat, perfect handwriting on my report card those many years ago—Hannah Clark, Homeroom Teacher, 7A.

"Welcome, welcome, Miss Clark . . . Hannah. Welcome to my band of angels. I know I am in for a quality education . . . for I am familiar with your quality work as a teacher." I silently sent the message on its way floating on the vibrations of love.

Hannah came into my writing on March 7, 1981, and left, without a word of warning or a good-bye, on my birthday, March 25, 1981. In just eighteen days, she filled thirty-two full pages of my angels' notebook with fascinating analogies, succinct wisdom, cogent advice, and interesting comment on civic and social concerns of this planet as seen from the angels' "expanded viewpoint."

She advised me to keep the eagerness for learning which is important for the growth of the soul; to always ask of my angels any thought that might seem confusing or fearful.

In the first major lesson of her transcript, Hannah lectured on man's relationship with others on this planet. *"Man seems to have pushed from his mind that others also dwell on this sphere. Consideration should be given to those with whom he meets every day.*

"All humanity is tied together with a common bond— individual spirituality or individual spiritual heritage. It is not found in some and not in others. No selective consideration has been dispensed.

"Imagine if that thread of commonality were a heavy rope binding each human on earth to the other. Some wish to go up, others down. Some wish to travel slant-wise, others wish to go back. Some wish to forge ahead while the laggards wish to lie down and go no farther. Chaos. A mild word for the situation, is it not?

"The world finds itself in just such chaos. The solution is: for those who go forward and keep their wits about them, those whose spiritual growth is recognized and nurtured, to accept the command. Urge the laggards, guide the wayward, inspire the dullards, and assure the timid.

"We shall continue at the next session. Blessings, Love, Hannah."

Were it not for the fact my arm ached miserably while my head swam with Hannah's rapid dictation, I would have asked her to continue the lecture . . . a far cry from my attitude in seventh grade.

At the second lesson the following morning, Hannah began, as usual, with the title of the topic, "Obligations and Duties of the Mortal."

"Each has a duty to himself," she informed me, *"but, unfortunately, this premise is vastly misunderstood and misinterpreted. The duty to one's self is not to feed each vain carnal desire which presents itself. The duty to one's self is not to destroy all that is good just to satisfy a vainglorious whimsy. One must slay the false self. Yes, slay the dragon of selfishness for duty to one's self does not recognize selfishness. One should develop* Selfness, not selfishness. *The difference between the two is vast.*

"The divine duty to himself each mortal must exercise is the obligation to one's true self, to expand his spiritual knowledge, to grow and to open his mind.

While writing, I thought about the messages I had heard many times from the other angels in my group of advisers. The same advice. Hannah quickly interrupted my wandering thoughts: *"Jesus repeated spiritual truths by packaging these truths in various parables,"* she said. *"We, too, must use every approach to underline the basic truths, to emphasize the utter importance of these spiritual truths.*

"I bring you knowledge in a different wrapping but underneath it is the same undeniable truth."

At this point in the writing, I chose to take a break. The muscles in my arm twitched from the speed of the writing. Hannah's words whirled in my mind. Dawn broke over the horizon beyond my window, as I checked the clock. Hannah and I had been communicating for more than a half hour. Try writing dictation fast for a half hour, seldom stopping. My eyes seemed to be jumping in all directions.

Rising from the desk, I walked to the patio window. Six resident cats, nearly evenly spaced around the pool, drank their fill, keeping a wary eye on each other, looking like a small pride of lions at an oasis satisfying their thirst.

Two mourning doves, flirting shamelessly, teetered gracefully at the roof's edge. Nature shook awake with a rustling of ficus leaves; the sounds of early morning stirrings of life filled the air. Taking a deep breath, I smiled. "Good Morning, God," I whispered. "Thank you for this beautiful morning and for my angels."

Once again taking up the writing, I heard Hannah immediately dictating, rapidly. *"God is the center of all things. At the same time, He is in all things and around all things. He is of all things.*

"The secret of life, the secret of the universe, is sought by all, each in his own way. Hundreds of thousands do not recognize their hunger; they deny their thirst. If man is offered a banquet of food, he may think he is satiated

but that is folly. Man is fooled more often by himself than he ever is by another mortal.

"Man chases illusory rainbows. He wastes his talent, he wastes his life. The secret to finding the divine rainbow is within himself. The abundant riches are within his soul. The wealth lies deep within and not in the bank of mortal thoughts."

Hannah's words in my ear became Miss Clark's words; the same tone, the identical vocal rhythm of my seventh-grade teacher as she gave her homeroom students the daily lectures. From somewhere deep in my memory, I saw her standing before me, her hands clasped at the waist, the pile of graying hair perched neatly atop her head, the voice soft, but commanding. In that moment I acknowledged the monumental amount of learning she gave me in those years and how that learning enhanced my life. My heart swelled with appreciation and love. Many questions filled my mind and I turned my thoughts back to the writing at hand. Hannah pressed on immediately.

"At the next session prepare questions if you wish to alter the subject of my lectures now. I read your thoughts but it must be you who presents them to me. In this fashion, by this method, we avoid confusion in transmission of answers. Do you understand the reasoning behind this request?

"You can look forward to greater joy, my young friend, and full abundance. Live the joy in your heart. Place it where it will be a beacon to all those who lose their way.

I am gratified of our association and we shall continue for some time. All send their most loving blessings to you and yours. Love, Hannah.''

Questions? You bet I had questions! I made out my list and presented them to Miss Clark at the next writing session.

"Why did Merlin write the book was finished when it was not?" I asked of Hannah.

I seemed to hear her soft chuckle as she replied, *"My dear child, you have yet much to learn. Some here are not infallible! Have you forgotten that fact? Some here are comparative newcomers on the path, you must remember, and are as capable as falling below standards on occasion as are you in your mortal schooling, although here never seriously, for we are closely monitored as to our responses so as to take a precaution against harming your education. However, we are allowed minor mistakes to learn by. If you more closely examine Merlin's words, could they not be interpreted otherwise? You took for granted that when he wrote 'it is done,' he was referring to your project when he may have been indicating the completion of his current tenure as your instructor. Is this not so?*

"You must remember that neither is the receiver infallible, and is perfectly capable of jumping to conclusions, do you agree? Many times, too, the medium neglects to listen closely enough to what is being sent. Is this not a possibility? Regardless of who perpetuated the misconception, the project continued, did it not, and with no damage done to

either side. Do listen more carefully and analyze the entire message before you deem it a positive answer. Your next question, please."

In my excitement and pleasure with Merlin, I may have heard wrong, or as Hannah put it, I may have misinterpreted a possible faulty transmission. Hannah had pointed out, firmly but not unkindly, a possible error by me. Properly enlightened, I wrote on the paper the second question: "When an angel leaves, exactly where does it go?"

"By this do you mean an exact location?" Hannah asked. *"If so, and I were to tell you the information as though it were a site on an unfamiliar city map, you would know no more than you do now, would you? If you had never been to a certain city and I said someone lived at the intersection of A and B thoroughfares, you would be no wiser as to his location as you were before you asked, now, would you?*

"Your guides go to other places on this plane where they are needed far more urgently. Because of your acceptance of the fast pace of your lessons, you free the angels for other duties much more pressing. You wish now to ask something further?"

My third question was this: "Is it possible for two mortals to have the same guide at the same time?"

"If by the time you mean at the same instant, no, for a transmission cannot be interrupted while in progress. During the same time span, yes. Time, you see, really has no meaning in our realm so we must translate and trans-

pose into your frame of reference. It would be possible for me to counsel you tonight and when we finished, I could immediately counsel another mortal soul in another place. On this level we do not indulge in idleness.

"Do you think we indulge in idleness and rest when our session with you is finished? Oh, no, indeed! Much time, as you interpret it, would be lost. Not that the time element is important to us, but demand for our services is great. You see, we counsel those who call on us but we also watch over those who do not. We must try to get their attention, do you understand? It is very difficult to counsel if we are not recognized for then we are frequently totally misinterpreted.

"William, Neven, and Merlin are within reach. They know of your progress. They may return to you at an appropriate time. They have not disappeared from this realm, but are on a different street, so to speak."

My next question concerned the guide of a friend of mine. "Is it possible," I asked, "for me to summon a guide from someone else?"

Hannah answered, *"You might be convinced that you could and believe that it is so. However, it would not be possible if you made the choice. Possible in your mind, yes, but not possible in the reality of things, you understand. Totally improbable if one guide is busy on a different level. To us none of this is at all complicated, but with the narrow limited use of the mortal comprehension, it is exceedingly mystifying, is it not? As we have told you before, ours is an expansive viewpoint while yours is not."*

After that profound statement, Hannah resorted to a wonderful analogy to put her point across, one that I have repeated many times to those I counsel.

"Suppose," Hannah instructed, "you were in the desert seated behind a rock. Your companion chooses to rest atop the rock. He sees a monstrous beast and shouts to you, 'Look at that monstrous beast!'

"You would answer, 'There is no such monstrous beast for I cannot see him from here.' Then your friend says, 'Look at the beautiful double rainbow on the horizon; and you look at everything you can see from where you rest. No double rainbow graces the horizon which you face, so you deny his statement. Does this not show you why it is difficult to accept some of our explanations and why you sometimes misunderstand our viewpoint?

"I think we shall conclude today's lesson with love, Hannah."

Chapter 18

Hannah left without a word of warning on my fifty-ninth birthday, March 25, 1981. With that last message, she simply vanished from the writing not to return for nearly three years.

In the interim, over the same three years, six new angels took up their posts to advise me in many ways, on many levels. In order of appearance, the names of the guides were Major, Marion, Angela, Adji, Catherine, and Ogden.

Each angel had its own special way of announcing itself. Each had its own style of transmission, of syntax used. The common themes of love, truth, choices, our relationship to God and others became the common thread of most of the messages. The vibrations from each angel differed, as personal and unique as the fingerprints of mortals.

MAJOR

Major identified himself as a college acquaintance, killed in a plane crash when in the army in World War II. Initially, his transmission left much to be desired. He seemed to be struggling to express himself. At one point, Major admitted to having unclear transmission and thought perhaps it was because he had strongly requested to come into my writing. Since I was someone he knew at the time of his death, it might be easier for him, he said; maybe he had come to the writing too soon.

Over time, his transmissions improved and he became capable of answering any questions my "clients" put to him. I had been a practicing psychic for some time, doing readings for strangers referred to me by others. I charged no fee but did accept any love offerings. Many blessings came my way in different forms: postage stamps, stationery, flowers, tickets to movie screenings, money, candy, leather notebooks, fancy pens, jewelry, and much love and approval. Those who came seemed delighted with the answers the angels conveyed to them through me as the medium. In many cases, my astonishment at the exciting answers given by my band of angels overshadowed the clients' amazement.

After a month or so, Major exited with this message: *"The glory of each day is absorbed and the feeling is one you wish all would share or could share, just as you wish all to share your knowledge. This is the way our program works—for all to share with others their knowledge of us and our work here. Mankind must know of us in great numbers and the mathematical progression of telling two and two each telling two and those telling two makes our work go so much easier and faster. Those who do not go abroad and share the knowledge with others is [sic] holding our program back. Always help others. Go out into the marketplace each day and practice all you have been taught else you do us a disfavor. Your project will be accepted and it is urgent that you work on it in some way every day. Tell the world of us as soon as possible. Love, Major."*

MARION

Marion, the next angel to make himself known, scattered French words and phrases throughout his transmissions. Because Marion sent messages at a high rate of speed and quite articulately, I never got around to asking him about the French.

After the usual compliments about my diligence in my learning and the assurance that I am blessed and loved, Marion started his lecture without a pause.

"Weep not for those who are less fortunate for tears are a waste. Give a river of love instead of a river of tears and send your concern to those who block their own path. Neither scorn those in their ignorance, but help them

learn. Those who are not ignorant, yet scoff are the losers, are to be pitied. Send many vibrations of love. You must keep those things in your heart at all times. Do not get short-tempered with those of great ignorance. Their day of reckoning comes.

"For all to join together to save the world, we must function in the light of God. You there must function in your association with others daily and must use all we give you in your walk through daily life. Ma chérie, each person, each creature, each flower, each shrub, each star is of concern. We cannot emphasize strong enough the need for all in God's army to get out into daily life and practice all we have given you. If you do otherwise, you do not help our work."

Marion stayed with me from May 7, 1981, until July 1, 1981. During that time he wisely counseled many of the clients who came to me for psychic readings. During his tenure as one of my guardian angels, he dictated sixteen pages of wisdom.

His warnings included keeping rein on one's temper; not being too quick to judge others; keeping one's thoughts above the mortal; not allowing one's ego to dictate one's actions; doing away with the "trash" in one's life.

In one passage, Marion sent this: *"Man is in control of his own destiny and cannot place blame elsewhere if things go awry. He has power to control his own life. If he fails, he must look to himself."*

Marion's topics included self-delusion, achieving

honesty in facing one's self, and the power of prayer, praise, and thanksgiving. His tenure ended with this analogy:

"With the naked eye man sees little of the universe. With a powerful instrument he discovers stars and planets he did not know exist for he could not see them with his mortal eyes.

"With the mortal intellect, the limited mind, man knows little of the universe. With Divine Love, Divine Truth, with faith in God and pursuing of God's light, man can discover the mysteries of life, glorious things he did not know exist. He did not believe because he could not see. Man must explore beyond the perimeter of his limited thinking to find the Divine Peace he seeks. There he will find a continual abundance of riches, for with God, the Spirit, nothing is impossible.

"You are blessed, ma chérie, hold all these things in your heart. Love, Marion."

ANGELA

July 2, 1981 . . . *"My name is Angela and I am come this day as your most recent guide, as a disciple of God to steady you in your faith, to encourage you in your love and help lead you up the path. I help light the way and go as a companion with you, but I do not perform the tasks you must perform for yourself.*

"God's light shines on you, my dear, and you must

never turn from it. Bask in the light of God, sing His praises. Look within in the silence and peace, for God is ever with you. Seek Him not in the hinterlands, although He, too, is there. You need not look away to far horizons, for He is as close as your own soul and it is there that you will find Him."

Angela, the once cloistered nun in a French monastery, who also informed me she had been my aunt at that time, introduced herself with the preceding speech, then promptly seemed to point a finger at me, warning me to be aware of my shortcomings. She reminded me that I do not always conquer the error and I should make a greater effort *"the next instance a formidable situation arises."*

The following day, Angela gave me encouragement about my shortcomings by sending this: *"The spark of spiritual understanding may slip from your consciousness but, once the first exhilarating awakening comes, the spark of divine understanding remains undiminished. The flame is merely hidden by a temporary barrier. You never lose the spark once you have experienced its glory."*

For two months, Angela showered her transmissions with poetic wisdom, chiding me now and then to keep on the path, to not get discouraged. She counseled my clients unfailingly, all the while giving me a wonderful education. At one point she ordered me to *"conquer yourself."*

In no uncertain terms she sent this message to one

of my "religious" clients: *"Theologians of fundamental religions sometimes limit a man's spirit. They teach of a wrathful God who punishes if you do not obey the laws of a particular denomination. This is not so. They instill guilt. This should not be so. A person's first regard is to himself—not the selfish personal ego or identity, you understand, but to his spiritual self and all other things fall in place in due course."*

Angela warned me several times she would move on, only to take up another subject and run with it . . . for several pages. On September 3, 1981, Angela told me she had an important point to make before she finalized. She sent this message: *"The division of Gentile and Jew is quite foolish. The Messiah does not mean only one person from alpha to omega. The Biblical Jews expected a long-awaited Messiah, not believing Jesus was the one. The Gentiles hailed Jesus as the one and only Messiah, not leaving room for the thought that God, at some point in the future may deem it necessary to send another Christ-like child of God to set an example, since mankind has not chosen to place the spiritual above all else. What foolishness for the Jew to deny the Christ (consciousness) of Jesus. It is a moot point they do not label him Messiah. What foolishness for the Gentile to think no other Messiah will ever be sent. Limited structured thinking of theological schools and temples and churches must expand to be effective.*

"God cares not if one is called Jew or one is called Gentile. God cares only for the growth of the soul. Any

secular division is an affront to God's plan. All men must strive to see God, all men must find the path. Their earthly identity is of absolutely no consequence.

"Think long on this and try to point out to others that earthly categories have no significance. All are God's children. Love, Angela."

With that, my guardian angel, the late French nun, disappeared.

ADJI

In September 1981, my husband, Ron, went on a jazz tour to Austria, accompanied by me and my new guardian angel, Adji. The name, he explained in his first transmission, has several meanings in different languages, but for me, he said, the name will indicate a gentle storm. Adji ignored the oxymoron and explained that, by the name, he would be forceful and insistent, but "velvet-gloved" about it all.

First, however, he dispelled any confusion about Spirit Guides. *"We as Spirit Guides do not replace God in your consciousness. We do not take away from your relationship with God nor God's relationship with you. He dwells within you and is the very core of your being. We come as His disciples to do His bidding, to help where we can and to explain where we can. Most of us are pupils also learning of God's great plan, of divine truth and love. We are putting our souls in order, just as you are. So never feel we are a replacement for God for there is no substitute for the Source of all being.*"

On the tour, because of our fast-paced schedule of concerts and sightseeing, I wrote very little. Adji did not care one bit. He just chattered a lot in my ear, guiding and protecting us from potential pitfalls during the entire eighteen days. Instruments were lost and found; we survived, without incident, a drive through fog along the Danube after midnight; unusual tourist opportunities opened up enabling us to see far more than we had planned. On our return to Los Angeles, Adji advised, with a purposeful attitude, yet with warmth and charm, all clients who came to me. Then, on December 1, 1981, Adji gave an advisory farewell speech.

"Praise each day the God within and seek to know the divine power. Be ever diligent in this for it is the secret of life and is the answer to all the world's problems, which, of course, have begun with the individual. Each person must seek this power if he is to attain all he wishes.

"Be aware that we are here to help you. Listen. Be ever alert for us for our contact is constant although your reception may not be so."

From October 3, 1981, until February 27, 1982, Adji guided, directed, commanded, praised, cajoled, and preached, not only to me, but to clients who asked interesting, serious questions of my Spirit Guide, astounded at the content of the messages.

Months before Adji arrived, I did not write daily,

at times letting a week go by unless someone called or came by for a reading. I began attending the metaphysical church more often in April 1981. I found it fascinating that my guardian angels came up with a phrase or a topic the minister presented in a sermon the following Sunday. I thought perhaps my guide of the week had been whispering in the minister's ear. I no longer believed in coincidence; everything happened for a reason. Then Adji bid me good-bye. His reason? His tenure as an adviser to me had ended.

CATHERINE

The day after Adji left, Catherine flew right in. *"Come fly hither and yon with me, darling child,"* she wrote, *"and together we shall adventure this way and that. We shall feel the joy of God surround us in the meadows as we play, in the skies where we shall soar and beside the babbling stream that flows through every land. Nothing shall hold us back from this joy, for the journey forward is all things and carries you from one great joy and blessing to the next. Can you now feel the elation, the lifting of the spirit to greater heights? We shall help others to find this true glory. Adjust yourself, balance and harmonize this night and with a joyful song, we shall be off on our adventure."*

And fly we did, from one topic to another; from

one consciousness to another. At one time, when my readings for clients became so numerous I could scarcely keep up, I asked a question of Catherine for a friend of mind. This friend asked about a Susan who lived in the San Fernando Valley. Catherine said I should ask myself why she concerned me and why I asked about her.

"I ask for a friend who asked for her daughter about the person in question."

Catherine seemed a bit miffed. She answered by asking, *"Would the answer make the spiritual life of any of these persons more advanced? Would any information help in the spiritual growth?*

"Our coming to help through this writing is just that, to help. All who ask must ponder why they are asking. Does it satisfy the curiosity of early events or personalities; does it reveal a divine plan for any or all? Earth lives could be wasted by satisfying curiosity instead of advancement of a soul."

Catherine, I learned, had been my seamstress whom I educated. She had come now to repay the debt . . . and guide my education. Her skill as a seamstress became the basis for a clever analogy in one of her interesting messages: *"Until one plans ahead for a major activity, there comes chaos,"* she wrote. *"When deciding to make a garment, does the tailor cut and seam without some guideline? No, it would be foolishness to proceed in such a manner if one wishes the end product to be successful. Decisions are made as to color, fabric, design prior to the laying on of the pattern. Then one proceeds with care and even stitches to fashion a suitable garment. One must reject inferior fabric, weak thread, and fastenings for a sturdy and lasting product.*

"Care should be taken every step of the spiritual way. Choose the best thoughts to meditate upon and throw away those which deter. Lay out the pattern of your desires and trace and cut them with care. Join all segments together with love and faith and the perfect raiment for your soul is wrought."

Although much of Catherine's advice echoed the same themes as the other guides, she had a different way of expressing herself at times. I never became bored with Catherine as I sometimes had been with the angels in the early stages of the writing. As I seemed to expand my consciousness, my angels appeared to become more articulate and more creative in their expressions.

"Regard each moment as the most important in your life, the most important in terms of learning, in terms of absorbing knowledge, in terms of giving, understanding, loving, and helping others. Be aware each moment of your spirituality and spread that over your entire day.

"Keep on your toes for many events are poised to begin rolling soon and you will be involved in many activities.

"Do be aware that each second of NOW becomes THEN—in the past—in the next second. We here do not especially concern ourselves with time, for the quality of life spent is indeed more important than its length. This

is particularly so in the area of spiritual growth, of spiritual evolvement.

"Living a quality life is joyful. Helping others, praying for others is quality of life. Acquiring knowledge and learning truth is joyful. Overcoming terror thoughts and actions in any degree lends quality to life."

The more I attended the metaphysical church, the more I realized that for the past couple of years, my angels in the army of God had been preaching the exact same philosophy as the church. The parallel proved more than uncanny. At the time, I considered it miraculous, as in rare, unique, or unusual. After I stopped the formal communication with my angels and studied more of the metaphysical philosophy, the connection with my angels remained, of course; but, on now with my angel, Catherine.

One day I asked Catherine if there were extraterrestrial beings. "We do often become amused at humans. Yes, of course, and anyone who uses his mind at all could deduce the answer. So many expect replicas of human persons or at least beings who have similar appendages, eyes, a nose, mouth, ears, head, torso, yet misshapen according to human measurements. Would the human believe there are many souls not in the earth environment? Yes, many extraterrestrials, many who are not at all in mass form but can create that illusion at will and who can do so for specific persons.

"There are many levels of Spirit Guides or angels who can make their presence felt strongly so that a human *actually 'sees' because of the strong vibrations and not because of a mass form. Thus the perfect illusion is created and the human does 'see.' Oh, yes, there are and more and more will be sighted in the near years ahead. There will come a time when the appearance will no longer be incredulous news. It will be commonplace. High velocity receivers will not be necessary for the natural currents of various active waves will carry thoughts from one to the other.*

"It is done now but is not yet a sophisticated form of communication. Heaven knows [it is] not accepted by the masses of mankind. That, too, will soon change. Soon only the narrow-minded and bigoted will remain stubborn in their beliefs. Others will be delicately led to rid themselves of the limited viewpoints. That joy is ahead."

The preceding message came through from Catherine on July 6, 1982. At this writing the year is 1995. No one can deny that in the last thirteen years, the average consciousness has expanded to include the possibility of active angels in our lives. Television shows, movies, and books about angels abound. The awareness of spirit entities has increased a thousandfold. The world is being candid and open-minded about those who make their transitions and, in their ethereal bodies, accept the assignments to help the mortals as the human beings hone their skills of communication.

Catherine bid me good-bye with this final message: *"It has been a [sic] much privilege to be your guide and*

*to see your progress, for that, you see, has also assured
mine. Blessings forever to you. Go on with eager anticipation and joy. Love, Catherine."*

OGDEN

The last angel to make itself known through my
automatic writing told a nasty little story of our relationship in a previous life long ago. Ogden's message
stated our relationship was one of "high intellectual
standing," but with nothing spiritual about it, at least
on the surface.

I will let Ogden tell you about it: *"During that span
we were not the least concerned with our souls, but were
more concerned with acquiring material knowledge and
writing of our findings. We were men at the time and
foremost in our field of linguistics at a small university
in the British Isles. Aloof snobs, you might say. We had
much to learn of the human condition.*

*"We cared for no one but ourselves. In our work, when
the deaths came a few short years from each other, we had
accomplished very little in either our spiritual or in our
chosen careers.*

*"Actually we had very little enjoyment at all as I recall,
but the events were stamped in our memories, such as our
lives were. After our transitions, we realized we had made
no progress in our spiritual growth and that in itself is
progress, is it not? To recognize one's faults points to*

*awareness which allows knowledge to enter. We have jour-
neyed a great distance to this point and together we shall
steer you to your next landing place in your education.*

*"Come, old girl, perk up and get yourself ready. We
shall not be complacent this time. There is much work to
do so get ready. All here watch with love and encouragement. Love, Ogden."*

Some of the work Ogden had in mind must have
been to serve others by giving readings for people.
At one time or another, as more people spread the
word from one workplace to the other, I found myself giving several readings a day. People also tele-
phoned with questions for the angel of the day, or
sent letters with questions they wanted answered
through the automatic writing. Between questions,
Ogden continued giving me sage advice.

"The discipline you need," he wrote, *"must be prac-
ticed to be an acquired habit. The evolution of the soul is
quite dependent on discipline because without such, we
could not focus our thinking on that which is best to save
us. Everyone should practice discipline, not only in that
which they very much like to do, but also in that activity
which seems such a task."*

I had a strong premonition that Ogden would soon
leave the writing. At each session I expected some
sort of farewell. When it came, no benediction of any
sort appeared, not even a signature. However, the
final message sounded loud and clear: *"You are the
soul of God and are universal in this, therefore when you*

speak the word sincerely through the soul, God hears and answers. This does not mean God hears with physical ears such as adorn each side of your head, but one vibratory force responds to another when attuned. You hear the vibrations of thunder because those vibrations reach the sounding board in your ear and you respond. The vibrations you send in sincere concern and prayer reach a universal sounding board, as it were, which responds.

"One must FEEL in addition to THINK to have success in this. On occasion, that is what seems to be a failure in getting prayers answered, one mouths and wishes but one must also FEEL to his very core, you understand."

Ogden, the last of my angels, disappeared from the formal writing never to return. Perhaps he continues to whisper in my ear without identifying himself. All of my angels do that these days. They continue guiding and protecting me and giving sage advice although I no longer write formally. I just listen. And heed. And give thanks to my guardian angels.

Chapter 19

❧

The decision to stop the writing did not come easily. I had become quite attached to my band of angels, eagerly looking forward to what new angel might surprise me next. Who would it be? What would it be like? Would it bring a new insight into my spiritual growth?

From 1982 on, I became more regular in my attendance at the metaphysical church. Then something happened that eventually changed my focus and direction away from the formal daily writing: I had a heart attack and experienced two angioplasty procedures and bypass surgery in one day. Evidently I had not taken seriously Mother's warnings about my health.

Because our trade union insurance had collapsed, and the new policy we had acquired not yet activated, we had no insurance to cover the expense. My bill totaled well over $52,000!

In the church I attend, professional spiritual counselors are available to help one pray in the right way to heal an adverse condition in one's life. I had not worked with a practitioner because I felt I might rely solely on the counselor and not do the proper work myself. I was wrong.

When I learned our minister, a wonderful counselor himself, had a practitioner, I asked him why he would need counseling.

"Because," he said, "I am human and at times, if a negative condition seems overwhelming, it is difficult to get oneself out of the way emotionally."

Before engaging the services of a practitioner, I consulted the guides, not knowing which angel might respond. "Are there words of advice for me at this time?" I asked.

"Believe with all your heart. Let nothing shake your faith or your ideals. Keep plodding and working to believe and sustain. There will be further activity and change in the year to come. Stay in balance and call on your belief and your faith in the Truth and you will understand all. We here send blessings and love to you. Listen in the silence and you will hear the wisdom of the ages. Love, Hannah."

Immediately I engaged the services of a practitioner with whom I had become acquainted a few months earlier. I liked her very much and felt comfortable with her. Through her wise guidance in counseling me, we were able to discharge the debt as paid in full in less than a month, just a year and a half after the surgery. With that demonstration I knew the angels had led me to my calling. I asked for the opinion of my angels in the army of God to be sure I traveled in the right direction.

One last time I called forth Hannah, and she responded, *"Let go of any fears and questions. Just KNOW! And be glad in the KNOWING. You learn more and more. There is not too much learning, you know. You will be joyful. Go! Love, Hannah."*

My husband and I became members of that church. I studied three-and-a-half years to become a practitioner. My angels led me the entire way. They pushed, shoved, shouted, smiled, laughed, and loved me into the marvelous life I enjoy as a professional practitioner. They sit on my shoulder and whisper in my ear as I counsel those who come to me.

I no longer have need for the automatic writing. The angels tell me the practice was a springboard to the work I do now. I have "graduated," they tell me, to a higher level on my path. They rejoice that this book is done. At this very moment I hear them telling me to start thinking about the next project. I always follow the advice of my Spirit Guides . . . Angels in the army of God.

Epilogue

Proverbs: According to My Guardian Angels

—Make each day count, for it does not repeat itself.

—Love is woven in the fabric of Truth.

—Open your mind and let the light shine into your soul.

—Focus your thoughts without scatter and learn to keep your mind in one place.

—You will know Truth by the light sent to your mind and soul.

—Open to the word of God and all things good come to you.

—Live each day by the light in your mind and soul.

—One cannot live for others. They must seek Truth for themselves.

—You cannot do all things until you learn Truth and Love.

—God sees all and knows all; keep His joy in your heart.

—A man who is caught in the web of this narrow material world and will not see the light, must go through (life) many times.

—Thinking a thousand thoughts at once is like stuffing all the food in the world in your mouth at once. It can't be done. Take each bite and chew it well so it gets properly digested.

—You cannot walk a mile at any time no matter how much you pray to do it until you initiate the first step forward.

—Let joy ring in your heart, open the gates and you will go forward on the path of light.

—It is never necessary to further your spiritual growth with elaborate rituals. Simple honest prayers constantly uttered, sincerity, faith, and love are all the ingredients one needs.

—God hears all and knows the sincerity of a person's desires.

—Kneel before no mortal man; pay honor only to God, the God within.

—Spread the word of God's light and love to all who are ready and willing to heed.

—Discipline your thoughts; do not let them wander to impossible lengths. Discipline is part of spiritual training.

—Faith and love are the things eternal life is made of—faith and love.

—Believe and love all things, no matter how great or how small.

—All souls carnate and discarnate must band together in the army of God to spread the word.

—Do not hide the light of knowledge under the basket of personal self, personal desires, personal feeling. Spread the joy.

—Each day on the earth is precious to enjoy, to appreciate, learn and grow.

—Do not worry if you are doubted when you talk or write of us. Everyone will know sooner or later. Keep to the path and you will find what you seek.

—One's mind should never get blocked by preconceived obstacles which hinder the flow like an iceberg damming the stream.

—If you have faith, doubts die away, error drowns in its own stupidity, and there is untold joy in the world.

—The good and the righteous will prevail in all conflict.

—Come always to the Lord and He will lead you out of the danger of straying.

—Keep faith burning brightly in your heart and soul and do not waver from the path.

—Open your soul to God, the Creator, in all you do, in all you see, in all you think. Keep these things in your heart at all times and feed on them for they are manna to the soul.

—Pray without fail each day and an answer will come to you.

—One must discipline himself if he is to see the path of light.

—Learn to live according to Divine Law, Divine Harmony, Divine Balance. To upset these is to court disaster.

—Believe that all will go well, have faith, never doubt.

—Always keep before you the idea YOU are the one, YOU and GOD, who get things done. In the final summation, it is YOU who is the instrument on which God's wisdom is played.

—The universe is there for any with like mind—the universe and God.

—Throw doubting thoughts out of your mind like garbage.

—Have love toward all things and many joys will be yours.

—God hears you and we hear you when you pray, when you ask, and when you wish.

—Do not fear anything, for we are here to guide and protect you.

—Be patient and persistent in your quest for spiritual enlightenment; function according to Divine Law and all your goals will be reached.

—Follow your hunches and intuition, for it will be us whispering in your ear with God's message.

—Do not for one instant drop the torch of Truth that you have lifted so high to light the way.

—You are in God's army to help anyone who is open to your guidance and wise counseling.

—Touch base with God each moment and all good things will be yours.

—Only your soul has substance and remains alive and functioning forever.

—Your interior is the heart of God where all things are perfect.

—Never fear. We are always here loving and guiding those who turn to God, the Creator of all there is.

—Do not let your faith waver. Believe that it will manifest, believe it will not waver.

—A relaxed mind allows more to enter than one fraught with tension.

—From where you are, your view is not as expansive as ours. We can see beyond the bend of the lane whereas you see only the part of the path as you look at your feet.

—Remember spiritual law. What you think, what you believe, what you say, you get in return.

—Genuine concern for others is a part of the growth of each soul.

—The army of God, of which you are a part, as are we, is continually working for the betterment of mankind.

—Love is the most important thing in all the universe—next to God, of course, but then God *is* love so it is of the same.

—Listen and you learn it is not such a strain to hear the word of God. Listen with your heart; listen with your soul.

—When you hear the beauty and uniqueness of the sound of God's words, from then on there will never be a doubt in your mind as to your human destiny nor the destiny of your soul.

—Get ye out to mankind and tell them of Divine Love, Divine Law.

—Keep your faith in God, in us your guardian angels, and in yourself.

—Tell the world we wait for each and all people of the world to open to us so we may help them. If they would but see the light, they need not be in such unhappiness.

—Tell the world we stand waiting and eager to come to the aid of each man, each woman, and each child.

—Look to God and you people of the world will at last know the joy which you seek.

—The material things of this world are soon lost and are meaningless.

—Homage should be paid only to God and not to man for one soul is no more or no less than the other.

—Never be in doubt for anything; ask and you shall receive if it is for your good and not ill.

—You must stay strong to help those who mock the Truth and lose their way.

—As you grow toward the light each day, your life will change, expand, and grow.

—The key to a good and happy spirit is to love all things.

—Keep love in your heart, love in your soul, and put away forever the petty things of the world.

—Gather your energies and work hard to see the light of God.

—The growth of the soul is the most important goal in anyone's life.

—The flesh is lost in a short time but the soul lives on.

—God is love. God sees all and knows all. No one can hide from it.

—Keep your mind focused and open to better hear God guiding you, through us.

—Only through God will you have a happier more fulfilling life in this university of the soul.

—What you do each day can be considered lessons in the life's school.

—Get into action to oil the wheels which can become rusty if not attended to.

—Faith without action is dead.

—There is but one path to the light—God. We are no more or no less than you with the same goal— to abide in God's light for eternity.

—Sweep all doubts from your mind to open the channel for God and His wisdom to come through.

—Keep love in your heart even when it seems difficult to do so.

—Love is the blanket that warms the soul.

—A man is fooled more often by himself than he ever is by another mortal.

—One should develop Selfness, not selfishness.

—Peace cannot manifest in the world until Divine Peace, Divine Love, is realized in each soul.

—Listen in the silence and you will hear the wisdom of the ages.